AFTER HOURS

UNIVERSITY OF NEW MEXICO PRESS *ALBUQUERQUE*

Lawrence Block [signature]

AFTER HOURS
CONVERSATIONS WITH LAWRENCE BLOCK

LAWRENCE BLOCK

ERNIE BULOW

To Mildred Goldfus, 1903–1994
—L.B.

For my brother, Barry Bulow
— E.B.

Library of Congress Cataloging-in-Publication Data
Block, Lawrence.
After hours: conversations with Lawrence Block / Lawrence Block,
Ernie Bulow—1st ed.
p.   cm.
Includes a Block bibliography and some previously unpublished pieces.
ISBN 0-8263-1583-6
1. Block, Lawrence—Interviews. 2. Detective and mystery stories,
American—History and criticism—Theory, etc. 3. Novelists,
American—20th century—Interviews.   I. Bulow, Ernie, 1948– .
II. Title.
PS3552.63Z462   1995
813'54—dc20   94-34718
                                                              CIP

designed by Linda Mae Tratechaud

CONTENTS

Introduction:
Greenwich Village Is the
Center of the Universe

LAWRENCE BLOCK is actually even funnier in the flesh than on paper. His quick wit and slyly droll sense of humor come across even better face to face than in his books, possibly because in humor dramatic timing can be everything and in conversation Larry doesn't have to depend on a reader to supply appropriate pauses, subtle emphasis, lifting inflection or the other nuances that sharpen and focus a clever turn of phrase. The leprecaunish grin—an Irish inheritance from a previous life—and his distinctive, raspy baritone voice certainly add to the overall effect. And behind the trappings of performance he has an intelligent mind, an almost encyclopedic combination of interests, an irreverent view of the world, and a singular disrespect for sacred cows. All of which, to my mind, makes Block a delightful dinner companion.

Several months ago, as I write this, Lawrence Block and I met Beth Hadas, director of the University of New Mexico Press, for lunch in Albuquerque. Beth wanted to meet Larry, who was in town to give the keynote speech at a writers' conference, and we all wanted to talk about our plans for this book. In the course of some scintillating banter, sandwiched between the mesquite-grilled free-range chicken breast and the vegetarian mixed grill (presentation is everything), mutual friend Tony Hillerman's name came up. His book *Sacred Clowns* was finally hitting the bookstores after a three-year hiatus.

This brought us around to "ghost" books—titles in various authors' bibliographies that never existed. Hillerman has *Mudhead Kiva*, the gift of an overzealous editor at Harper Collins, Block has his *Guidebook to Australian Coins*, my old friend Edward Abbey had *Rock Salt and Cherry Pie*, which was the working title of *One Life at a Time, Please*, and even I have one—a pamphlet on Dorothy Johnson, the writer of western stories ("Hanging Tree", "A Man Called Horse"), which I was supposed to do years ago for the Boise State Western Writers series. These titles get perpetuated when one bibliographer cribs from another, and collectors find these books especially desirable and elusive.

It turned out that Block once had a ghost book he laid to rest by writing it several years after the fact. Before starting his eponymous imprint, Donald A. Fine was the publisher at Arbor House. Poking delicately at what I hoped was merely seared zucchini, Larry told us the story:

"Not long after *Eight Million Ways to Die* was published, I got a call from Arnold Ehrlich, then my editor at Arbor House. He said Don Fine, the publisher, wanted to know something about the next Scudder novel. 'I don't know,' I said. 'I don't know if there'll be another.'

"'God, don't even say that,' he said. 'Of course there will. Look, just give me a title, something I can rattle off at the meeting.'

"'*Like a Lamb to Slaughter*,' I said.

"A while later I got another call from Arnold or a minion, wanting some plot information about *Like a Lamb to Slaughter*. By then I'd made an attempt at a sixth Scudder novel and gotten nowhere with it, and was feeling rather hopeless about the whole thing. I said something to this effect, and asked why such information was needed, anyway. I think whoever it was mumbled something about a sales conference. 'Well, somebody gets murdered, I suppose,' I said. 'And Scudder investigates, and does something about it. It all takes place in New York.' Wasn't that true of all the Scudder books? 'You bet,' I said.

"Next thing I knew the title was listed in the Arbor House catalog, with a generic description and a scheduled publication date and everything. This would have bothered me more than it did, but Fine made a habit of this sort of thing. If he could stand it, so could I.

"Then, a couple of months later, the book was reviewed."

By now everyone at the table had lost interest in the mesquite-seared free-range rutabagas in chilipotle sauce.

Larry was grinning at us. "Now that was a surprise. A reviewer in one of the men's magazines wrote about several new mysteries, one of them *Like a Lamb to Slaughter*, featuring Matthew Scudder. The plot summary was a little vague, but the reviewer made no secret of the fact that he had enjoyed the book and found it a worthy successor to *Eight Million Ways to Die*. 'I think this is a good sign,' I told my agent. 'All those years of writing books and not getting reviewed, and now I'm not writing books and getting them reviewed, and a damned generous review at that. I like it better this way.'

"I eventually met the reviewer and found out what happened. He was frustrated by the magazine's long lead time, which often led to the books being off-sale by the time his reviews ran. Accordingly, once in a while he would take a chance with a series book by a writer whose work he had always enjoyed in the past. After all, if I had a new Scudder novel coming out, and if all the earlier Scudders had pleased him, he wasn't exactly going out on a limb to praise the new one, was he?

"He hadn't counted on being sabotaged by Fine's overly optimistic catalog.

"A few months later there was still no book, and it was clear to me I wasn't going to be able to write one, not for a while if ever. By now Don Fine had left Arbor House. I went to Eden Collinsworth, his successor, and pointed out that it had been a couple of years since they'd done my short story collection, *Sometimes They Bite*. I had enough stories for a new book, and would take a token advance in the interest of having another collection on the shelves. 'What we'd really like,' she said, 'is another Scudder.' I admitted I'd like nothing better myself, but it didn't seem in the cards right now. 'We have a Scudder in our catalog,' she said. '*Like a Lamb to Slaughter*.' I said I knew that. There was, I said, a Scudder novelette which could be the collection's headliner.

"Eden thought for a moment. What, she wondered, was it called. I reported that it was called "A Candle for the Bag Lady." 'Hmmmm,' she said. 'Could it be called "Like a Lamb to Slaughter"?' 'Jesus,' I said, 'that was perfect for it. Why hadn't I called it that in the first place?' She gave me a look. 'All right,' she said, 'We'll do the collection.' 'You can't go wrong,' I said. 'It already got its first rave review.'"

As soon as we all stopped laughing I said, "Damnit, why didn't you tell that story during the interviews?" to which Larry replied, with a huge grin, "You didn't ask the right question."

I have a feeling I didn't ask a lot of the right questions. I have the feeling that I could tape another eight hours of conversation with Lawrence Block and still not have him run out of interesting things to say. But for now this book is what we've got, and a delightful treat it is for Block's many fans.

I first met Larry under auspicious circumstances. In 1989 I had just done a book similar to this one with Tony Hillerman, and on one of my visits to his home Tony happened to mention a gathering of mystery writers to be held in Key West in January. When I looked into the conference I discovered that one of the organizers was Les Standiford, who had been a graduate student at the University of Utah the same time I was. Les now has a couple of mysteries under his byline. Not only that, another Utah alum, Jim Hall, had just published his first mystery, and it was being well received; he was also living in Florida these days. As it turned out, the gathering was a who's who of the mystery field though Lawrence Block was not one of the participants.

It was an incredible experience to meet so many legendary authors in such a congenial setting and, as it happened, my last chance to experience a couple of them. Charles Willeford, who was finally receiving long overdue recognition, died only a couple of months later. John Ball of *In the Heat of the Night* fame passed away within the year. There were a lot of emerging talents as well. Carl Hiassen's second book, *Double Whammy*, had just come out.

At dinner one evening I sat next to the great editor Joan Kahn, who had been responsible for so many fine books, including the Tony Hillerman series. Other famous agents, editors, and publishers had gathered, and the crowd was so gilt-edged I can't remember if there were any civilians there or not. One of the people I finally met in Key West was Dennis McMillan, publisher of offbeat first editions and limited hardcover reprints of authors like Willeford, Hillerman, Crumley, and Fredric Brown. I had dealt with him by phone and fax for years and in Key West we seemed to spend a lot of meals together, along with mutual friend and book dealer Maurie Neville.

The last day of the conference we were joined at lunch by Larry Block, and I've already mentioned that he's up there with Groucho Marx in the bon mot department. It was an enjoyable lunch, probably free-range shrimp and mesquite-grilled snapper, and I gave Block my business card and told him to drop by, as though New Mexico were an afternoon jaunt. A couple of months later he and his wife Lynne did just that, and I got to take them to the West End Deli, one of Gallup's few decent eateries, where the ambience is pure New Mexico. There are plenty of Navajos at the tiny tables, state cops hitch at their Sam Browne belts menacingly while a variety of construction types knock the mud off their work boots. The sandwiches are wonderful.

This was during the time the Blocks were doing their stint on the road. They were heading for a month in Sedona, Arizona (I think this was before the Harmonic Convergence made Sedona the in place for crystal gazing). In the years that followed we crossed paths at several Bouchercons and similar gatherings and I started collecting Block's earlier works, a somewhat difficult task these days. Before our meeting in Key West the only Lawrence Block I had read was the Tanner series way back in the sixties, so I had a real treat when I discovered Bernie Rhodenbarr and Matt Scudder, not to mention several collections of witty short stories.

When *Talking Mysteries* was nominated for an Edgar it surprised every-one, especially the University of New Mexico Press, which had produced a first printing of only 3,000 copies. They took the book on only because someone believed in the power of Tony Hillerman's name to peddle books. I could sell the idea of an ongoing series of similar conversation books with mystery writers if I could deliver one or two really big names. The only really big name I knew personally was Larry Block. I wanted to go to New York anyway, but I had the idea that I could pitch a project best face-to-face. So two years ago at the Mystery Writers of America awards banquet I proposed putting together this book and Larry expressed inter-est in the project. We talked—where else?—in a famous Manhattan deli and I got the valuable intelligence that an egg cream is made with neither eggs nor cream. I never know when that kind of information will come in handy. It took another year, and another MWA meeting, for us to actually sit down in the light and airy Chelsea apartment of Lynne Block's pal Joan Scherman—with the ubiquitous sound of sirens and car alarms floating on top of the constant street babble—and actually tape the interviews.

In the meantime I was reading through his considerable body of work as I was able to lay hands on some of the more elusive titles. At the same time my friend Jim Seels of ASAP Press was working on a Block bibliog-raphy, which he has allowed us to borrow from generously here. Even minimal research raised some interesting questions about the various Block pseudonyms. There was no problem with the irrepressible *faux naif* Chip Harrison, or the darker voice of Paul Kavanaugh, but there was a definite problem with names like Sheldon Lord, Andrew Shaw, and Jill Emerson, just three of more than twenty *nôms de plume* according to Block's own count. Jim kindly sent me a copy of the essay Lawrence Block had written about the subject for his bibliography.

The problem is a simple one—in a sense. Block, who does hundreds of signings and appearances a year, is sick of being presented with stacks of old paperbacks which he may or may not have written, but which the obsessive fan expects he will cheerfully autograph. Though we talk frankly in the interviews about his writing apprenticeship, the subject of pen names was one of several areas which turned out to be forbidden territory. Jim Seels and I—and any right-thinking fan with an ounce of sensitivity—respect Block's wishes to let this undeserving pulp rot in paperback hell. But . . .

Larry Block has made a number of references to this period, these books, and even the pen names in some of his nonfiction writings. He has talked about the collaborations with long-time friend and fellow author Donald Westlake, and it is common knowledge they co-authored at least two books, *A Girl Called Honey* and *So Willing*. Block's hilarious *Ronald Rabbit is a Dirty Old Man* draws on his days writing soft porn, and Westlake's ribald spoof *Adios Scheherazade* and Hal Dresner's *The Man Who Wrote Dirty Books* are both novelizations of the authors' years with sleaze-factory fiction.

Westlake has spoken openly on the subject, as has Dresner. Sci-fi authors Marion Zimmer Bradley and Robert Silverberg were also part of the group. For a detailed exploration of this whole topic I refer you to the paperback catalogs of bibliographer extraordinaire and soft-cover expert Lynn Munroe of Orange, California. Lynn and several of his paperback-dealing cronies have devoted untold hours—way too many, it might seem—to the sleuthing of Block pseudonyms in the Bedside Reader genre and have uncovered some interesting material. Munroe and company have used internal evidence to bolster their conclusions; references to Block's college and an old college roommate, dedications to various members of the group as well as Block's relatives, the title *A Sound of Different Drums* which was apparently started by Westlake and used by virtually everyone, and other strange and sometimes obscure points. What really amazes me is that they actually *read* all this stuff. I showed Larry a Lynn Munroe list devoted largely to him, and he read through it with apparent relish, grinning widely as he nodded yes and no to the entries. Unfortunately, I wasn't looking over his shoulder, so I can't put the record straight. He declined to comment on specifics, but admitted that at least some of Munroe's assumptions and conclusions were correct.

The truth is, I don't really have any interest in proving the authorship of any questionable titles, exposing any more of Block's pen names, or even spurring any more interest in this quaint and dated genre. What is interesting to me is the cameraderie and high spirits this group displayed—the sense of humor they shared, the iconoclastic stuffed-shirt bashing they did, the practical jokes they played (Larry tells the true story of the famous poker game in the interviews), and what a great training ground this otherwise odd body of writing proved to be.

One of the most delightful pranks they ever played Larry declined to comment on. According to Munroe—and I'm sure he's right—the entry for John Warren Wells in *Contemporary Authors* is the only one dealing with a totally fictitious author, and, though Wells seems to be a Block creation, I don't know which of them wrote the supposedly autobiographical entry. As a prank, however, I think it ranks with the famous case of the fraternity boys who were working a chimpanzee through a degree at a major university. As I recall, the chimp's grade point was better than mine.

Jim Seels and I commiserated with each other about our failure to sway Block from his ban on discussing the pen names, and both of us settled for simply acknowledging that we knew about them but were deferring to Larry's feelings on the subject. Now Block tells in his latest newsletter that he is about halfway done with a booklength exposé on the whole subject. I expect it will be a major treat for Block fans when it appears.

During my off-and-on career as a journalist I have probably done more newspaper and magazine articles on artists and craftspeople than any other category (except movie reviews perhaps). Having been influenced by the "new journalism" of Hunter Thompson and Tom Wolfe I like keeping interviews loose and unstructured, eschewing prepared questions (though I usually couldn't have done much advance preparation anyway, my subjects being even more obscure than myself). Vanity being what it is among artistic folk, and the need for publicity being what it is in the creative world, most subjects are so eager to be helpful they'll tell you anything they think you want to hear.

My favorite setting for an interview has traditionally been a bar, or at least a restaurant, on the theory that a full stomach or a few drinks puts an interviewee at ease. It also gives the two of you a chance to get acquainted and comfortable with each other before the serious talk starts and defensiveness gets a chance to creep in. I am notorious for not taking many notes, let alone taping the conversations, but my subjects have never yet objected when I quoted what they meant to say rather than their exact words, bad grammar and all.

When I interviewed Tony Hillerman I was, of course, drawing on some years of friendship and shared experience, but I was also simply keying into some set speeches and stock anecdotes which the master storyteller had buffed and polished over the years as a veteran journalist himself, and hardened interviewee.

The biggest problem I had with the Walter Satterthwait interviews was that Walter and I share such a common pool of likes and dislikes, favorite authors, and pet peeves that we were constantly wandering off the subject and drifting into unprintable attacks on anyone or anything, or simply philosophizing on the nature of nature, and the role of the doodle bug in the Great Scheme of Things. Enjoyable but not very productive.

Though Larry Block was exceedingly generous with his time over a period of more than a week, not counting the hours we spent together on the streets and in the coffee houses of Greenwich Village, I had not prepared correctly for the interviews. Though I had read as many of his books as I could lay hands on and a wonderful autobiography Larry had sent me that I wish we could reprint here, I expected simply to wing the interviews as I normally did. I was not confidently briefed, arsenal of questions at hand, with a solid idea of how my subject was going to react to certain questions and lines of inquiry. As it turned out I struggled and sweated considerably during the eight hours of taping, talking myself into corners and box canyons on several occasions.

There were three areas of Block's life and work which turned out to be totally proscribed, though he was reluctant to talk about his personal life in general on the grounds that it wasn't relevant to his career as a writer, and wasn't anyone's business in any case. He simply wouldn't talk about the pseudonyms at all, and a few references which crept past were later deleted. He refused to talk about his films, though he said it was something he was constantly asked about at signings. And I didn't get anywhere when I tried to gently probe the subject of alcoholism, which is so central to the Scudder books, structurally and psychologically.

A slightly grayer area had to do with things like his work habits and the general subject of writing technique, which he has discoursed on in a regular magazine column and three books, as well as the seminars Larry and Lynne ran for several years. People tell me that Block's books on writing are the best and most useful available and I concur with that assessment. If I asked a question Block had covered elsewhere it tended to get short shrift.

I soon discovered where the forbidden areas lay; I had known about the pen names before we ever got together, of course. But, egoist that I am, I was sure I could get Larry to talk about anything at all if I just approached it right. Not. Then again, maybe I just never found the right approach. The point of all this is simply to explain that the book is not exactly what I set out to put together and the dearth of material on, say, Block's movies isn't the product of ignorance or neglect on my part.

I felt that in our rambling conversations we had gotten some really good stuff on alcoholism and that aspect of the Scudder series, but Larry exercised his rights as interviewee and cut that material from the final transcription. I never dared ask him to share his personal demons with me and the reader.

The problem of the films is more mysterious to me. The first movie adapted from a Block novel was *Nightmare Honeymoon*, a 1973 film starring Dack Rambo and Rebecca Smith from his book *Deadly Honeymoon*. We don't talk about it here. Years later Jeff Bridges and Rosanna Arquette made something of a muddle of *Eight Million Ways to Die*, my personal favorite among the Scudder books and a pivotal novel in the Block oeuvre. Whoopie Goldberg changed a Jewish gentleman cracksman from New York into a black female cat burglar from San Francisco without any obvious improvement to plot, character or setting. None of that was her fault, probably. The film was called simply *Burglar* and a workman-like performance by Sam Elliot couldn't take the edge off the adenoidal ranting and frantic twitching of Bobcat Goldthwaite. Anyway, we don't talk about either of these films.

Not surprisingly, Lawrence Block has tried his hand at screenwriting (a trade far more lucrative than the authoring of novels) but without much success to date. He told me he tried a screenplay of *The Thief Who Couldn't Sleep* which didn't sell, and the third Kavanaugh book, *Not Comin' Home to You*, was originally drafted as a screen treatment—that being more than a short story but less than a completed script. Block admits he is constantly barraged with questions about the films at signings, but we didn't talk about any of that.

Undoubtedly the real treat in this book for most fans will be the four previously unpublished nonfiction pieces included here, along with a reprinting of Larry's first published short story, which we talk about at great length in the interview. Novelist, anthologist, and collector extraordinaire Bill Pronzini was kind enough to supply me with a photocopy of "You Can't Lose" from the February 1958 issue of *Manhunt*. Since we talk so much about sense of place and the role played by journeys in Block's life, the two travel pieces need no introduction.

The humorous sketch "A Modest Proposal For the Categorization of Mysteries" is a small satirical gem which will be best appreciated by writers and fans who have been involved with Bouchercon, Mystery Writers of America, and the various fan organizations which give out a bewildering array of awards each year. At this point Larry has won so many honors himself that they are nearly impossible to keep track of. By my count he now owns four Edgars, the first Nero Wolfe Award, and two Shamuses and is the only person to win two Maltese Falcons, a mystery award given by the Japanese. There must also be some Anthonys and McCavitys. He can make fun of awards if he wants to. If you've never read Swift's "A Modest Proposal" I suggest you look it up first to fully appreciate Block's sense of humor.

"Outliving A Father" has special significance for me because my own father died when I was ten and he was thirty-seven. I have long since passed that landmark, and it seems younger to me every year. Some people are lucky enough to delay their confrontation with mortality until middle age, but some of us, for one reason or another, find ourselves haunted by the spectre of death and thoughts of our own demise from an early age. The story is a rarish glimpse into the personal life of Lawrence Block, and I like it very much.

Larry and Lynne are, as discussed at some length in the interviews, confirmed New Yorkers who live in the Village. They had just found and purchased an apartment there when I visited for the interviews. It has a wonderful view to the south toward the financial district and the towers of the World Trade Center. To the West the apartment overlooks the lights along the Hudson River and New Jersey. It is just around the corner from the old meat-cutting district and St. Bernard's of Scudder fame.

I had timed my trip to interview Block to culminate with the Mystery Writers of America awards banquet. During the awards ceremony Block picked up an Edgar for best mystery and introduced his longtime friend Donald Westlake as the recipient of the Grand Master Award. Both of them are witty and delightfully entertaining, and the evening seemed to be the perfect cap to my trip. I thought at the time that the two men's careers are so parallel they could have switched roles.

It was no huge surprise that Lawrence Block was named Grand Master at the 1994 awards show. I hoped that Don would be tapped to make the presentation, but Larry's old friend, editor, and agent, Knox Berger, did the honors. Though Berger is not a big name to many of today's mystery fans, he has been influential as the editor of *Argosy* and, even more important, the Gold Medal Books line of paperback originals.

Block noted that it was Knox Berger who sold his first book (under his own name) and "He just sold it again. That's the kind of agent I like."

Larry was witty and charming, and a large part of his talk was about his first job in the book world and the publishing of his first short story, pretty much as it is told in these pages. Noting that false modesty was the only kind he had, he said he hoped his future wasn't all in the past, which is often the case by the time a writer is so honored by his mystery writing colleagues. Not only is Block the youngest writer to be named Grand Master, he seems to be at the height of his literary powers and has recently revived Bernie Rhodenbarr after a long hiatus as well as adding to the Scudder canon, seeing his first Tanner book issued in hardcover, and planning a couple of story anthologies following the careers of Ehrengraf and Keller. (And don't forget the autobiographical book about his early writing career.)

After the banquet the Westlakes generously invited me to their house in the Village to join the Blocks and some other writers in an after-hours wind-down from an evening where Larry got yet another Edgar—for best short story. Otto Penzler was at Westlake's with his well-deserved Ellery Queen award for lifetime achievement in the mystery field as critic, editor, publisher, anthologist, and general promoter of the genre. It was a wonderful evening and I got to eavesdrop, so to speak, as the big boys talked about current projects, copyright laws, movie adaptations, friends, and enemies.

Maybe I can talk some more writers into books like this. In the end they are a lot of fun and their own reward. Oh, I almost forgot. Bernie: I've got one of the best cases of Morton's Foot you ever saw so I know how you feel. Hang in there, kid.

The Interviews

ERNIE BULOW When did you first realize that—for better or worse—you had a predisposition toward being a writer, that the literary life was the life for you?

LAWRENCE BLOCK That's easy to remember. It was in the eleventh grade at Bennett High School in Buffalo, New York, and we had to write an essay for English class. That year I had an English teacher who liked my work and was very responsive, and accordingly—perhaps consequently—I enjoyed flexing my muscles a little in the papers I wrote. The encouragement that I got from her put the thought in my head—gave me the idea of becoming a writer. That was also the year I began reading extensively in contemporary realistic fiction—the great novels of the American twentieth century.

I read a lot and, besides being excited about the writing, found myself identifying with the writers and decided that writing was what I wanted to do. I began by writing poetry and little essays, and I simply knew that I would eventually be a writer.

EB Who were the writers who were capturing your imagination?

LB I'd always been a reader, and earlier on I read a lot of the juvenile classics and some mystery fiction. I read what was around the house. But in high school I began reading people like John Steinbeck and

15

Thomas Wolfe and James Farrell and Hemingway and pretty much the mainstream of American realists.

EB   How did you discover this marvelous body of literature? I wouldn't suppose you had to read those writers in high school English class. Most schools don't teach anything significant at all.

LB   No, no. Nobody read that in high school. It probably started with something I found around the house. I read a novel that particularly struck me and my Mother said, "If you like that, you'll probably like so-and-so." My parents were both extremely literate and well read.

And while there were a fair number of books always around the house there was also library access, and I just read and read.

EB   One author would lead to another?

LB   That's right.

EB   Do you remember specific books that had an impact on you?

LB   No, not specifically. When I found a new writer I liked, I would read everything he had written.

EB   So you didn't go through that phase where you read, say, Jack London and wanted to go to Alaska?

LB   No, that wasn't my kind of fantasy. As I already said, I was just reading and reading. I was a very big fan of James T. Farrell, for example, but when I was reading his books I can't say they ever made me want to go to Chicago. But what all the books I read made me want to do was to be a writer.

EB   Do you remember what it was that drew you so powerfully to the idea of writing? The romance of art, the power of language, the magic of imagery, impressing the girls? I don't suppose you had some vision of writing as a way to be rich and famous, so much as some other lure.

LB No. Certainly not the idea that writing was the way to be rich and famous. Only in recent years, I think, has that come to be the spirit of a lot of people's writing fantasies, now that we're in an age where the news stories focus on the big numbers and the fat advances, rather than whether a book is any good or not.

I don't know why writing called to me. I felt, I suppose, that this was something I could do and something that was pretty much worth the doing.

EB I remember reading probably as much *about* Hemingway as Hemingway's work itself, and being more impressed, perhaps, by Hemingway's self-created macho image and adventurous life-style than his actual words. While he may be an extreme example, I believed that most writers lived in exotic places, did exciting things, had women, money, adoration. I didn't hear about the hard work, isolation, frustration, and other realities of the writing life until much later, though some of that must have suggested itself when Papa took himself out with a shotgun. Did you have a sense that it was a glamorous life, being a writer?

LB I don't remember. I think it was just wanting to do it. I should say, wanting to be a writer rather than having some story I was burning to tell. Some writers have absolutely no problem deciding what they're going to write, because there is something within them yearning to come out.

Some writers start right away with a rush of autobiographical material. Others may write something that is not demonstratively autobiographical that way but fabricate a story, some inner world that wants to be on the page, have a life of its own. I felt nothing like that. I don't know whether it was a blessing or a curse, but it had a lot to do with the kind of writer I became, because I had to spend quite a few years finding out what stories it was meant for me to tell.

EB So how did you make the shift from writers like Hemingway and Steinbeck to humorous fiction and mysteries?

LB Well, I don't know that I ever made the shift. I just started writing, you know. I really started writing during my first two years in college. I wrote a fair amount of short fiction and poetry.

And the first story I sold was crime fiction, although I didn't think of it as that when I wrote it. I just thought it was a story. I was in New York when I wrote it. This would have been the summer of '56 in the first co-op job I had up there my first year at Antioch. I was working as a mailboy in the mailroom at Pines Publications, which was an outfit that published a handful of pulps; they still had a few pulp magazines and Popular Library, that was their paperback imprint.

I was living in the Village and I was doing a little bit of writing but not a hell of a lot. There wasn't a great deal of time that I didn't have better things to do than sit at a typewriter.

But I did get what I thought was a great idea for a story. My stories at that time tended to be about three pages long with some sort of little hook at the end or some such slice of life to them. They were awful, of course, in that respect.

This was a story about a young fellow who was living by his wits and who had a variety of mail-order scams going and things like that. The story didn't really go anywhere, but there was some life to it when I finished writing. I went back to college in the fall and somewhere along the way I had read Evan Hunter's collection of short stories *The Jungle Kids*. Most of the stories had originally appeared in *Manhunt*. It was a good magazine at the time, although I didn't know that because I had never seen it.

When I looked at the story I had written, I thought, well, maybe I should send it there, because I had been sending things out to other publications to no avail. So I mailed it off to *Manhunt* magazine, which I only knew as the source of the stories compiled in *The Jungle Kids*. I found the address somewhere. I still hadn't seen the magazine.

I got a note back from the editor of *Manhunt,* Frances X. Lewis was his name, and it said, "This is quite good but it doesn't really end, it just trails off. If you can work up a good ending for this we would like to see it again."

Well, it was astonishing, this kind of encouragement, so I quickly ran out and bought the magazine. And I read a bunch of the stories and they were good stories. I thought of an ending for mine where this fellow who's been conning people one way or another is really going to get rich and is falling for a larger kind of scheme. It was an equivalent of O'Henry's "The Man at the Top"—that kind of ending.

So I rewrote it and sent it off to them and shortly thereafter got a letter back saying, "Sorry, this really doesn't work. It's kind of predictable and clichéd, but thanks just the same."

The following summer I went up to Cape Cod. I had my own plans at that time, and I decided not to take the job that the school had found for me. I went up to Cape Cod and I holed up in an attic and got a subsistence job as a dishwasher—which I quit after the first day because it was a horrible place.

And I was holed up in this attic at a rent of eight dollars a week and living on Maine sardines and peanut-butter sandwiches, and I wrote a story a day while I was there. In the course of driving across to Cape Cod I'd gotten an idea of how to fix that original story and how to put an ending on it that would work. And that was one of the first things that I wrote that summer.

I sent the new version off to *Manhunt.* I got a letter back almost by return mail, saying, "Mr. Lewis is on vacation right now," signed—I forget who it was signed by—but adding, "We think this works and we're fairly certain he will take it when he comes back." I was elated, you know. So I'm writing a story a day and I kept that up until I ran out of money, and then I decamped.

A month later I was back in New York—I had cracked up the car trying to drive back to Buffalo—living in a rooming house on Nineteenth Street, and I got a job at the Scott Meredith Literary Agency.

This turned out to be a wonderful thing for me. The agency was a real sweatshop in certain respects, and one of the things they had was a big fee-reading business—I think maybe they still do—where people sent in manuscripts and paid a reading fee. The fee reader's job was to write a letter over Scott Meredith's signature, explaining how the manuscript was extremely promising and all of that, but this particular story was flawed in certain respects—like the plot—and it didn't work but please send in another story and another fee. They would string these would-be writers along as long as they possibly could.

It required a surprising amount of ability to be a fee reader. You had to be able to write a good letter, in the first place, which disqualified a tremendous number of applicants. You had to be able to analyze a story sufficiently to pick out what was wrong with the plot, according to some formula, even though what was really wrong with the story was that the person simply couldn't write. You could never say *that*. You had to find some structural reason to send it back, along with some word of encouragement to keep them going.

Well, they were always trying to find readers able to do this and do it quickly, because it was a volume operation. So they had this test that you took in order to be hired on there. So I took the test. I was really too young, but they didn't much care. I think I had just turned nineteen.

I took the test and I sailed through it. I had had a writing course in college, and I'd been doing a lot of writing myself. The test consisted of reading a story that Lester Del Rey had written which purposely incorporated as many structural flaws as he could think of—a story called "Rattlesnake Cave"—and you had to do one of three things: one, write a letter saying this story is terrific and we're taking it out to market; two, recommend changes; or three, explain what was wrong with it. And I'd had enough training so that I hit all the structural flaws, and I was hired. I was also fast. That has always stood me in good stead. I've always been able to write rapidly.

So I was hired, and in those days there were only about five or six people in the office, except for Scott and his brother Sid, in various back rooms. The rest of us were in a sort of bullpen there.

Henry Morrison was working there at the time and was delighted when I was hired because I was the first person younger than he was in the company. So the bullpen got together and decided to have, you know, a little fun with the new kid. They were talking back and forth about *Manhunt* and what a rotten magazine *Manhunt* was, hoping I would chime in with something one way or another.

At this time—and this was still a secret—Scott Meredith was editing *Manhunt*. For years John J. Cloud had been the editor of *Manhunt*. Now the new editor was Francis X. Lewis. Neither of these people existed. It was Scott Meredith. This was manifestly a conflict of interest, because he packed the magazine with work from his own clients and all the rest of that. But that was what was done, and everyone at Scott Meredith was sworn never to divulge this.

EB There was recently a similar stink about conflict of interest with a major Hollywood talent agency.

LB Of course that sort of thing is still done, but this was very much the case there, and it was not generally known in the field. There aren't that many people even today who know that Scott was anything behind the scenes.

So Henry is saying this and that, and I chimed in and said, "Listen, don't knock *Manhunt* because I sold them a story." So Henry thought this was an outrageous lie and he slipped off into the back room and looked into the inventory. Scott was, at this point, on vacation, and Henry discovered that the story was in the file and they had indeed bought it. The letter I'd gotten saying the editor was on vacation was because they were stalling in order to avoid paying. They wanted to wait as long as possible to pay contributors because the publisher was having cash-flow problems.

So Henry came back out and said, "I'll be a son of a bitch. You really have sold 'You Can't Lose.'" He was elated about that. And then Sidney Meredith, Scott's brother, came up and took me aside a little later and said, "We have your story here and we want to buy it for *Manhunt*, and, incidentally, the fact that we edit *Manhunt* is a secret and you cannot divulge it and if you ever do, we'll deny it."

I'm fresh out of Buffalo and I didn't know what he was talking about. Then he said, "The story is two thousand words long. We would normally pay sixty dollars. However, here," he said, "here's a form. You sign this and you'll be a client of the agency." I signed it, and he said, "All right. Now you're a client of the agency. So instead of paying you sixty dollars we'll pay you a hundred."

And he said, "We take 10 percent." That was my introduction to the writing business. That's how I sold that first story. And as I said, it was a crime story. But that certainly didn't mean that everything that I was going to write was going to be crime fiction.

But that seemed to be where I got most of my ideas and what I most often wrote and what I was most comfortable writing. I don't know that there was ever a time when I said, you know, I am a mystery writer now and forever. I don't know that I've said that yet.

EB At nineteen years of age, what were you drawing on for inspiration? Where was the material coming from? I mean, you couldn't have had much experience. Very little experience in the world of crime, for sure, a nice boy from Buffalo.

LB Oh, no. It was imagination, certainly.

EB I know Flannery O'Connor is quoted somewhere as having said that anybody who survives childhood has enough to draw upon for a lifetime of fiction writing.

LB But I don't know what I was drawing upon. I think for many years my work was, if not specifically derivative, I think it had to be influenced by the things I read. I don't think it was until the first Tanner books that I was writing anything that was uniquely mine.

EB I've read that you were a very good student in school. Was that just because it came naturally or because you worked at it?

LB Well, I wasn't a good student. I did well in school. I got good grades.

EB That's what I meant.

LB I was a lousy student. I was bright and I was retentive, but I never did learn how to study. I don't know what that is.

EB So you got good grades because you were playing the game or just because it was easy to get good grades?

LB It was just easy. I was always good at tests, you know. It was just easy. I enjoyed school well enough through high school, I think. College, not so much. By college there seemed to be too many other things I wanted to do rather than suffer the academic life. I wasn't good at that.

EB I don't know much about Antioch, except that it's a fairly unusual school. How did you happen to go there?

LB My parents had heard about it, and it sounded to them as though it would be a place where I would enjoy myself and maybe find something of value.

EB Antioch isn't structured along the same lines as most traditional universities, isn't that right?

LB Yes. The thing with Antioch was that you spent half your time working in jobs that presumably had some relationship to your educational interest, and the school had a whole co-op plan to find you the jobs.

On-the-job training. But the jobs were, if anything, actually self-liquidating. You didn't save money toward college. It would cost you at least as much as you were going to earn to come and live in New York for three months, for example. But it gave people more life experience than they would get on a college campus, and more vocational experience.

EB How was the year structured? I mean, they obviously didn't have regular semesters.

LB No. It varied. They changed the summer program in the course of my career. Basically, it was a quarter system, and half of the student body was on campus at any given time.

EB I thought Antioch's emphasis was liberal arts, but apparently you could major in anything?

LB Just about anything. They had a very good record for getting premed students accepted in medical schools, for example. They had a good business department. Antioch certainly had an avant garde reputation. But I don't know, really, how much that was deserved, in that a large proportion of the student body was very straight. There was a very interesting mix there.

I think it probably did me good to have gone there, and I think I'm kindly disposed toward the school, but, it's very difficult to know. It's hard to know what I would have been if I'd gone somewhere else and if it would have made any substantial difference.

EB What caused your disillusionment with college? Was it just because these other things seemed more compelling, or were you feeling that it really just wasn't practical, wasn't truly useful?

LB No, it wasn't that. I was impatient. When I was working at Pines Publications, the fellow who headed the Promotion and Publicity Department approached me because his assistant was leaving for somewhere else. He didn't know that I was planning on going back to college at the end of the summer, and he offered me a job as his assistant. And I said, "Oh, I'd been planning on going back to college." He said, "Oh, for heavens sake, go back to college. Don't take this." And my inclination then was to jump at that job. I wanted to be doing things.

EB Did you have a specific major or course at that time, or were you just sort of dabbling around?

LB No. I hadn't decided on a major. And then, at the end of my second year of college, I got the job at Scott Meredith. It was just immediately clear to me that this was far more of an opportunity than college was, and I dropped out to keep it.

After one year I'd had as much as I wanted of the agency experience, and I did go back to school for a final year. I was interested in writing seriously by then. The last year I spent at Antioch—my third, after one year off in New York—I assigned a very low priority to the academic side of things.

I was by that time writing professionally. I had written and sold a couple of novels, in addition to probably fifteen or so short stories. I was in a position where I could earn a living writing, and I certainly felt that what would help me as a writer would be to write, not to spend my time reading Trollope, which may or may not have been true in retrospect. It seemed very clear at the time. I think for me it was clear.

So I finally did drop out for the last time at the end of the third year. At that point I would have had one year more to go to graduate. I can't say I've ever felt the lack of a degree. It may actually be true that not having it has been of some curious value, in that I've never had anything to fall back on. Writers are so often advised to have something to fall back on. If you don't have something to fall back on, you can't afford the luxury of falling back. So maybe that keeps you better focused or a bit more dedicated.

There was a Gold Medal writer, a terrific writer named Peter Rabe, who wrote mostly during the fifties, I think. Then he stopped writing and disappeared, and I didn't know if he was alive or dead. But he surfaced a few years ago, and it turned out that he'd written for a while and then he'd had this psychology degree to fall back on, so he fell back on it and became a psychologist. Now, if he hadn't been able to do that, God knows what he might have written, because he was pretty good, you know.

EB I can think of a number of fine or promising writers who dropped out. Think of all the great books we've lost. Not to mention the good writers who don't have the stomach or the stamina to get published in the first place.

LB   Yeah.

EB   Actually, I loved that Gold Medal line. There were a lot of really good writers who published with Gold Medal, especially in the hard-boiled genre—from Octavus Roy Cohen to John D. MacDonald to David Goodis. And Louis L'Amour, for goodness sake. And a young guy named Lawrence Block.

LB   That's right. That was where my first book—well, the first book I did under my own name was with Gold Medal. The first several.

EB   Ahearns's *Book Collecting* lists your first book as one of those titles by Ard, *Babe in the Woods*. I wanted to ask you about that. You only finished the book, right?

LB   That's not a secret or anything. It was in 1960. I was just married and living in New York on West Sixty-ninth Street and I got a call from Henry Morrison, I guess, at Scott Meredith, saying that their client, William Ard, had died and one of the things that they thought need not die with him was a book that he was working on. He had two chapters and some sort of rudimentary outline of the rest of it. He had a contract for it with Monarch, and they wanted to know if I would finish it for the unpaid balance of the advance.

It was a rush job. It wasn't that great—the two chapters were not terribly interesting, and God only knows what I wrote after that. I can't imagine that that could have been any good, either.

I later found out that they went on with the books under Ard's name—Scott Meredith also specialized in the "living dead," as you might say. There were a couple of more books by Ard that hadn't been partly written or even contracted for that came out under his name. I won't say who did a couple of them, but it definitely wasn't William Ard. Some other writers did those, but I just completed that one.

EB   Had you read any William Ard at all?

LB   I think I read a book or two somewhere along the line, but they must not have been too memorable. You know, this was a third- or fourth-rate house called Monarch. If Ard was reduced to writing for Monarch, things probably hadn't been going that well, anyway.

EB   So you didn't try to mimic his style or anything like that?

LB   I just tried to write the book.

EB   So it's really your book, more or less.

LB   I wouldn't think so. I wrote it in the space of about a weekend. Somebody at Monarch claimed to be in a great hurry for it. I don't think they were. And though I was following the outline, such as it was, I'm sure I didn't know what I was doing and it must be awful. I can understand your curiosity, but I can't imagine anybody voluntarily reading the book.

EB   So when you published the first novel under your own name, you already had published novels under several pseudonyms?

LB   Oh, yeah. When the first book under my own name, which was *Mona*, came out in '61, I had probably written ten or a dozen books, which, you know, I'm not uncomfortable talking about but I don't like to identify because, as I said, I don't have any feeling for them. They weren't written to endure. It wouldn't bother me if they ceased to.

But *Mona* itself was a book that started out to be my monthly book for the paperback publisher of this anonymous work. And after I wrote the first chapter or two and felt that it had a voice and a life to it that was better than I had been doing and too good to waste, I decided to try and write it as a novel, with the intention of sending it to Fawcett.

And I wrote it and it went over there and they took it, you know, which was gratifying. But I had a funny thing about it. I suppose it was some sort of a lesson in itself, but it was difficult for me to write intentionally for other than a minimal market. So that over and over in the early years, the books I sold to better houses were books originally aimed somewhere else that I thought better of. *Mona* is just one example.

The second book I did, which was published under the god-awful title of *Death Pulls a Doublecross,* was another example. That one, I was commissioned by somebody at Belmont to do a tie-in novel for a television series called "Markham," starring Ray Milland.

So I started what was supposed to be a hack job, and when I got all the way through, I thought, "Gee, this is pretty good. This is pretty good." Belmont was only paying a thousand dollars, and that was the end of that. It was a tie-in and gone.

I think I asked Don Westlake to read it. He read it, and he said, "Yeah. This is pretty good." I sent it over to my agent, and he said, "Yeah. This is pretty good." We sent it over to Knox Burger at Gold Medal and explained the story and said we could change the guy's name to something else. He made a revision suggestion, and we changed the name of the lead character from Ron Markham to Ed London, and that was my second book. Then I still had to write a book for Belmont, because I had this contract to fulfill.

EB To turn out the Markham book.

LB Right. When I did the book for them, there was never any danger of anyone's thinking it was too good for the market. I did that same thing a few times over the years—upgraded a potboiler for a better market—and having sold to a better house, you'd think I would have always tried for that. Gold Medal was a wonderful market, and having cracked it, I should have been trying for that level with everything I wrote.

But something always stopped me. I would find myself incapable of coming up with ideas for Gold Medal books. I could only get there—

EB Accidentally.

LB Accidentally, yes.

EB That's interesting. I confess I've never read any of the sex books, so I can only imagine what they're like. I probably should have read some of them, but there is, as you know, considerable controversy about who wrote what. What I want to know is how you came to write them. I'm curious about the market itself.

LB Was there a regular formula, you mean?

EB Right. Where did the genre come from? Where did the books themselves come from? You were pretty young, and you weren't living such a bohemian life, after all. And some of the books attributed to you were pretty clinical—the "doctor" books.

LB But they had sex in the Village. Sex is everywhere. Just takes a little imagination, after all; how much more do you need, for heaven's sake? They weren't all that kinky or anything. Pretty tame by contemporary standards.

EB Like I said, I haven't actually read any of them.

LB I still haven't killed anybody, and Scudder has—I've done a lot of things in novels that I'll never do in real life, and I'll never know for sure if I got it right.

EB Still, I assume that there was an already established formula for the soft-porn books at the time, wasn't there? You had a genre to work from, didn't you? There was already a market in place when you got involved?

LB No.

EB No?

LB There wasn't. That was the interesting thing. When I first got an assignment to do one, that was a couple of months after I left Scott Meredith and before I went back to Antioch that summer. Summer of '57 or '58, it would have been. I got a note from Henry saying, "I hope you know what a sex novel is and how to write one, because if you'll send in three chapters and an outline, I think we can get a contract on that."

I didn't quite know what they were. The only publisher like that around at the time was an outfit called Beacon, and I'd looked at some of those, and what it seemed to me was that there was no particular formula, just a strong sexual element to the books and an otherwise ordinary story line.

But the thing is, there was nobody around but Beacon, and there were these other publishers just beginning to move into the field and I was one of the first writers for them, so whatever the genre formula was, a handful of us determined that by writing it. What we wrote is what that genre turned out to be. We made it up as we went along.

EB So where did the market come from? Who knew there would be buyers? This would be the fifties, right?

LB Late fifties.

EB Late fifties, and the first real testing of so-called First Amendment rights. I was growing up then, coming of age as we say. I clearly remember the *Lady Chatterley's Lover* trial and so on and so forth. You think some enterprising publishers were just taking advantage of liberalizing attitudes to cash in?

LB I don't know. I don't know where anything comes from.

EB These weren't underground publications? They were sold on regular newsstands?

LB No, they weren't underground. They were available everywhere. They had somewhat general distribution. As I said, they certainly weren't terribly hot stuff by contemporary standards.

EB They weren't pornography.

LB No. And that made it a very useful learning experience.

EB Who did you imagine they were aimed at, or did you know? Did you ever wonder who read the books?

LB Who cared?

EB It must have crossed your mind—"Who's reading these things?" you know?

LB I don't even remember it crossing my mind, to tell you the truth. It may have. I didn't imagine that Susan Sontag was reading them. They weren't operating on a terribly high level. However, you know, more interestingly, now and then, was what they did for those of us who wrote them. It was a very good school. It was a terrific apprenticeship if you were fast and if you had the guts to do it at all. If you were fast, you could make a living.

And you could write almost anything. It was an enormously forgiving form, as long as there was some sexual content to get things in focus every twenty pages or so. Where the story went and how well it was resolved didn't matter. You could use any character you liked; you could play with any background; any number of narrative-type things. You could learn an enormous amount, and you were not operating without a net. You were safe whatever happened, you know, as long as you got your obligatory sex scenes in at the right intervals.

I never had a book turned down for not working as a novel—for not having the right plot. They always worked. So you got to get a lot of crap out of your system, in terms of writing technique. I probably wrote more of them than I absolutely needed to for my artistic development. Generally, one tends to do things too long. That's how you find out that it's time to stop.

EB Well, were there any assignments? Specialists? I mean, did somebody write sexy Westerns and somebody else write sexy mysteries?

LB No, no, no, no. They were just books. They were contemporary novels with a high sexual content and, you know, they were designed to be readily comprehensible. But beyond that, there was a considerable amount of range possible. You could do anything you wanted.

EB Do you have any idea what the print runs were? How many were sold?

LB No, I don't, and we didn't really get royalties. We got a flat rate. Well, I don't know, the publisher got rich, so I think we did all right.

EB Did you ever look for your books? Check on the newsstands?

LB Oh, sure. Well, they were all over the Times Square stores. I don't know what their press runs were, but they did pretty well. And a lot of stores marked them up.

EB They sold them for more than the cover price?

LB Uh-huh. And over the years I taught people how to write them and used those people as ghosts, and, as I've said, one reason I don't really want to acknowledge pen names is that a lot of the work under my names was not necessarily mine.

And even in the absence of that, the publisher frequently switched names inadvertently, you know, because they were sloppy. There was one house where they overedited everything so that it wasn't anybody's work. A couple of times I wrote a book in a weekend. But I don't make it a secret that I did a lot of books in the factory system that way.

EB You wrote a hundred of these, altogether?

LB I don't know.

EB Something like that.

LB I quite honestly don't know how many. I know I wrote over a hundred books during that period, but I never actually figured it out. I don't know how many books I've written. But, you know, I don't care. It's not important.

EB How long did that period of writing go on?

LB Not that long.

EB I didn't mean just for you. Those publications, the "bedside reader" series? It seems like it was fairly short-lived genre.

LB   No, they went on a long time.

EB   Did they?

LB   I started writing them in the summer of '58, and one of those houses was still going and I think somebody was still ghosting under my pen name in at least '65.

EB   That's only seven or eight years.

LB   That's a long time for a phenomenon like that. And there was a time in the sixties when they reissued some of the early ones, with heightened sexual content spliced in, you know. Suddenly, they could use—

EB   More words.

LB   They could use more words, so they stuck them in, yeah. Of course, I won't acknowledge those pen names, for God's sake. But all the while I was doing this, I was writing books, and that was the important thing.

EB   And occasionally some of those plots would transcend the genre and you would have a real novel. One you felt you could put your own name on.

LB   Yeah. And there were also books that I set out to write as crime novels or whatever. They got written.

EB   When did you take the job with Whitman?

LB   I was writing the quickies first in New York. Then, after my first daughter was born, my wife and I moved back to Buffalo. That would have been in the spring of '62, I think, that we moved back. My daughter had been born in the spring of '61.

I kept writing the "one-a-month" books in Buffalo, and then sometime in '63—late '63—I had a falling out with Scott Meredith. They dropped me as a client, which closed a batch of markets to me, because they were sort of closed shops. Some of the sex-novel houses. So I found a way to do other things. I didn't go out and get a job. I thought of other ways to make a living writing. I had various houses in New York that I was writing for. But I felt sort of stalled in my career at that point.

One of the places that I found to write for was a new coin magazine that the Whitman people in Western Printing in Wisconsin were putting out. I did several articles for them.

EB Had you ever collected coins?

LB Yes. I started collecting coins and I got interested in the subject, and that's how I started writing for Western.

EB Had you collected as a kid?

LB No, not as a kid. Probably '60, '61, I got interested. I probably had a childhood coin collection the way everyone does—it didn't amount to anything—but I got seriously interested in the early sixties. It was really my chief extracurricular interest at this point.

A fellow from Whitman came to town specifically to look me up and to offer me a job with them. It didn't pay much of anything, but, for one thing, it was a way to get out of Buffalo. My wife and I had moved back after my father's death. We felt some obligation to be there and to be with family and all that, and I realized early on that that wasn't really where we wanted to be. It didn't fit, you know. And it was certainly a dead end in terms of career. I wasn't meeting anybody or getting anywhere that way. The one thing that the Whitman job offer would do was get us out of Buffalo. It did, and it got us to Racine, which wasn't necessarily an advancement, but, you know, Racine would be awfully easy to leave when the time came.

I had a good time at Western. I was good at what I did. I did not only the articles for the coin magazine and editing of that and putting that together but I did a lot of, oh, sales letters and advertising. I took over all those areas, really, in the coin division. Someone else had been doing it. And I found that very interesting and challenging, but I also knew that wasn't what I wanted to spend my life doing. I was a writer.

While I was in Racine, I wrote a couple of books. I wrote a book called

The Girl with the Long Green Heart, which wasn't bad. And I wrote a few other pseudonymous things for markets that I had developed; probably two or three books along that line.

And then I wrote the first Tanner novel. By the time I did that, I don't know if I'd given notice, but I pretty much knew that I was going to be moving back East and leaving Western.

EB   You knew the first Tanner book was a turning point then?

LB   I thought so. Anyway, that was my stint at Whitman.

EB   That was really the only time in your adult life you had a nine-to-five kind of tie-and-white-shirt job?

LB   Well, I had had short-term jobs. Of course, the year at Scott Meredith had been nine to five. Outside of free-lance writing, it's the only work I've had since college.

EB   Did you actually wear a white shirt and tie?

LB   I wore a white shirt and tie and a jacket every day. I got up at six in the morning every day, because it was a midwestern eight-hour day, which was a quarter to eight to a quarter to five. I got up every morning around six. One day about four months before I left, I don't know whether I didn't have a white shirt or just felt rebellious, but I put on a blue shirt. No one in the company ever noticed. I wore a blue shirt that day and no one said anything. And the next day I wore a yellow shirt and nobody said anything. And the next day I wore a blue shirt again and nobody said anything. And the day after that I don't remember what I wore, but everyone else in the office wore a colored shirt. And no one ever said anything to me or anybody else, and that was the only rebellious thing I ever did there. If you wanted to call it that.

The whole thing was surprising to me. I thought I would have trouble with the role. I thought I would have trouble hacking the whole thing—a straight job in a midwestern town—and I didn't.

EB You didn't find the routine tedious?

LB Oh, it was tedious, somewhat. It was a lot of hours to work, and I was tired at the end of the day. But no, I enjoyed it, and I was—I was much better at it than I would have guessed I'd be.

EB During that time, when did you write? How did you find time to write?

LB Nights and weekends. As I said, I did only a few books during that time. I was there for a year and a half.

EB You had to really want to write to add that to a full-time job.

LB Yeah. That's true.

EB Of course, you were already doing it. So that made a difference.

LB That's right.

EB What made you finally decide to leave Whitman and Racine, Wisconsin?

LB Nothing finally made me decide, really. I think it was just a realization. I never took that job with the intention of staying a long time. I figured a couple of years. And things started to open up in my career. The Tanner book that I wrote sold. *The Long Green Heart* sold. Another book that I had written somewhere along the line, a book called *Deadly Honeymoon*, sold after it had been knocking around for awhile.

Henry Morrison, who had been at Scott Meredith, had gone out on his own and approached me, and I'd gone with him, you know, so I had an agency connection. And I realized that where I wanted to be was back East and what I wanted to be doing was free-lancing, so I gave notice and left.

I don't think they were surprised. I think people who knew me knew that what I really was, was a writer. And they shouldn't have been surprised. We moved to New Brunswick, New Jersey, and I wrote books.

EB   Why New Jersey?

LB   Why there, specifically? Well, now, let's see, Henry Morrison may have already moved to Princeton, then. He had lived right down the block from where we bought, and Don Westlake and his first wife were around the corner, so it was an area where we had friends, and New Brunswick was about forty-five minutes by train from New York.

We were used to houses at this point, and I know we never considered moving right back to the city. In retrospect, I wish we'd done that.

EB   So you had the Tanner series started?

LB   I had the Tanner series started, and I'd sold my first hard-cover novel, called *Deadly Honeymoon*, which I'd written in Buffalo before we went to Wisconsin. It took a while for me to get into the mystery genre. That was a tough time for mystery fiction. In fact, the book after *Deadly Honeymoon* was a book called *After the First Death*, and that one didn't even get into paperback for years. Most hard-cover mysteries didn't at that time. Very, very few did get reprinted.

We were in New Brunswick for a couple of years. Then we moved to a country place, about a mile in from the Delaware River in western Jersey. Then in '73 the marriage ended, and I moved to New York and, with brief departures, have basically been here since. I was gone for a couple of years. After Lynne and I got married, we thought we'd like to be some-place where the living was easy.

EB   And you had your "time-on-the-road" period.

LB   Yeah. We moved to Florida, and after we were there for about two, two and a half years, we realized we didn't want to be there. I've always had a propensity to just go drive around or take buses around or whatever. I've made rambling trips like that quite a few times in the course of my life.

We'd had fantasies ever since we first got together about taking that kind of a long, rambling trip, and Lynne and I both knew we didn't want to stay in Florida, and we didn't know if we wanted to move back to New York or not. She had had a bookkeeping and accounting practice that she sold preparatory to our move down there. We didn't know if we wanted to come back to New York. We weren't quite sure yet, at the time. We didn't know if we might find someplace that we'd rather live, so we decided we would never have a better time to fulfill this fantasy of just living without a fixed address. We did that for two years.

EB I know some of the places you went, because you came by my place on your way to Sedona, Arizona.

LB We drove all over the country, you know, and we were in Sedona for, I think, a month. And the following year, we were in Santa Fe for about six weeks, and I think that's the longest we stayed anywhere. A lot of places—most of the places—we were only in overnight, you know. Some for a day or two.

EB You kept on the move. You were still able to write during this period?

LB No, not very much. When I would want to write, we would hole up someplace; in Sedona, in Santa Fe. The piece for the autobiographical essay, we took a suite in the Hotel Irma in Cody, Wyoming. Wonderful place.

EB One of my favorite bars. It was supposedly given to Buffalo Bill by Queen Victoria. The hotel is named for Cody's daughter.

LB It's a great place. So we stopped there, and I spent a few days writing that piece. It didn't take very long.

We just knocked around at our own pace, and a couple of times we went to writers' colonies, where I got work done.

EB Were there any parts of the country you didn't do? Did you make it to the Northwest?

LB Yeah, yeah. We got pretty much all around. The only place we didn't really get into that trip was New England.

EB So in effect, this was one long trip, your journey of discovery?

LB One long trip, really. It lasted two years. As I said, there were inter-ruptions—an occasional month in Florida, and there were a couple of trips overseas during that two-year period. But it was really two years without a fixed address. Two years of getting our mail forwarded to us by my eldest daughter and things like that.

EB Did a lot of good material come out of that, or were you trying not to think like a writer for a while?

LB Well, it's funny. I tend, you know, to travel as much as I possibly can. I roam all over the world and then come back and write books set in New York. The other tendency I have is to do my research after I've writ-ten the book.

I'd written a book called *Random Walk* in '87, and then six months later we took off on our ramble around the country. And indeed, we did retrace some of the route that the people used in *Random Walk*. But, you know, it's a strange kind of research when you do it that way; when the book is already on the shelves of the stores.

EB I recently read the interview that you did for *Sober Times*. It dealt with you and James Lee Burke and how you have both crafted best-selling mystery series starring recovering alcoholics who are based on your own experiences. Do you feel like talking about that at all? It's relevant to your career as a writer, after all, and central to the Matthew Scudder books.

LB Well, I don't want to talk a whole lot about it. You know, it's not a secret that I used to drink and that I don't anymore. But beyond that, I don't think I want to get into it.

EB I never got the sense that you were a really hard-core alcoholic. How bad did it ever get? I mean, what was the worst?

LB Well, if it hadn't had gotten bad, I wouldn't have stopped.

EB So it was pretty bad sometimes?

LB Yes.

EB What are your thoughts about its effect on your writing? There's a sort of legend in the literary world that a huge percentage of great writers were alcoholics and that they wouldn't have written anything great—that perhaps they couldn't have written at all—except when they were drinking. I don't even need to mention the names that come immediately to mind. But it's a common theme, actually, a common thread among writers and creative people in general. But in reality, it seems that we know that alcohol is something that really impairs a person rather than inspiring greatness.

LB I don't think there's any question that alcohol has been responsible for the decline and termination of more writing careers than anything else in the world. There is also no question but there's been an astonishing incidence of the combination of alcoholism or heavy drinking and writing—an extraordinary coincidence. I think they used to say that there were only two ways for an American to get a Nobel Prize. He had to either be an alcoholic or be Pearl Buck.

My taking it to whatever extent I have wanted is that, perhaps, some of the same elements that incline a person toward writing also may make them a set-up for alcoholism. However, I don't think the booze ever helps the work.

What it does in so many cases is lead to a certain degree of arrested development. Writers get to a certain level and then they stop evolving, growing—their work doesn't get any better or any deeper because the drink shuts it off. Even if it doesn't deteriorate, it just shuts it off. You don't feel like growing.

EB It has become so much a part of the legend. The tortured soul, the sensitive loner, the outsider, numbing the pain with alcohol. Creative people in general seem to share the problem. One of the standard excuses is that writing is such a solitary thing. You know, so lonely. Of course, there's all sorts of excuses.

LB I've heard a variety of people from various occupations talk about how this applies to them. A house painter says, "Of course, house painters have to drink. It's part of the job description." You know—but, of course, librarians have to drink.

EB Cops. Any stressful occupation, I suppose.

LB Yeah, right. Or non-stress.

EB How much effect on your writing was that having at the time you quit?

LB I don't know. You know, it's hard to—

EB Was there ever a time you weren't productive? It seems to me that in your bibliography there's something of a gap in the early seventies. Maybe you wrote under pseudonyms at that time.

LB Well, yes. In the early seventies, there were a couple of Chip Harrison books which were not published under my own name at the time but since have been. There were a couple of Paul Kavanagh novels that were not under my own name, but not because I disavowed them or anything. I took them as seriously at the time as the ones that were under my own name. It was just some sort of marketing decision at the time.

EB Have there ever been times when you *weren't* able to write for any reason?

LB Yes, but they haven't really been extended. There have been times when nothing much has come out that's been any good or things have gotten snagged one way or another.

There was a time in the mid-seventies. Starting in the summer of '75 there was a strange period of time for me. I had a lot of things go wrong in my personal life, and I wound up taking a long rambling trip. I drove from New York to L.A. It took about nine months to get there, you know, writing as I went along.

I did write a book during that time, and it did ultimately sell. It was *Ariel,* and I ultimately rewrote it substantially when it was finally published in '80 or '81. I had false starts on a lot of books. I don't think there was ever a time where I didn't write anything for a long stretch of time, but there have been times where nothing much came of it.

I had written three Scudder novels in '74 and '75—or maybe they were all in '74, I'm not sure. Then between them and *A Stab in the Dark,* which came out in '81, I think I had three or four times when I wrote twenty or thirty or forty pages of a Scudder novel and it just died on the paper. They just didn't quite work, and, in fact, one of those turned into the first Bernie Rhodenbarr book. The basic plot element—the idea of a burglar on the run for a murder that had already taken place before he had broken into an apartment—that was an idea for what would have been the fourth Scudder book, except I wrote forty pages and decided it was garbage and threw it out.

But I still liked that idea, and later I tried it again. I had him be the narrator instead of a client of Scudder's, and it was utterly different. There was no correspondence between the character of Bernie Rhodenbarr and the character that I'd had in the first version. But that was where the idea came from.

EB Back to that long, rambling trip. You took nine months to get from New York to L.A.?

LB Well, I wasn't in a hurry.

EB What was that like?

LB Well, let's see. I drove down to the Outer Banks. North Carolina was the first place I stopped, and I stayed there in a place called Rodanthe for a month, living on what I pulled out of the water.

EB Giving you the story "Sometimes They Bite."

LB As a matter of fact, and a few other stories. I wrote short stories as I went along. There was, as I said, no time when I wasn't writing.

EB What was your daily routine like at the time?

LB Well, I didn't have a daily routine. I really don't even have one now, when I'm living in stable circumstances. When I was in Rodanthe my routine was very simple. I went out on the pier and fished all day. Every day. That's what I lived on.

EB Thought about things?

LB I don't know if I thought about things. I've made a career of going through life never thinking about things. I don't know what the hell I did. But I caught some fish and there were some stories. I drove on and I stayed places for awhile.

EB Sleazy, cheap motels?

LB Yeah. I stayed in St. Augustine for—long enough to write a draft of *Ariel*. That's where the first chapters of that got done, after having attempted to write a draft. I worked on it some in Charleston and Jekyll Island and different places and couldn't get anywhere.

I sort of kept drifting and finally got out to L.A. and then holed up at a place called the Magic Hotel in Hollywood. Yeah. That's where I wrote the first Bernie Rhodenbarr book, *Burglars Can't Be Choosers.*

EB You talked about the origin of the plot. How did you come up with the character of Bernard Rhodenbarr, gentleman burglar, purveyor of used books?

LB I never know where anything comes from. When I sat down at a typewriter and I wrote the first chapter, I had absolutely no intention of writing a light book. All I knew was the idea of a burglar breaking into a place where somebody's already dead and the cops walk in and he bolts and runs and has to solve the murder to save his hide. That's easy.

On the first page, Bernie surprised me by coming to life on the page— and with an attitude and everything that I hadn't had consciously in mind. You know, sometimes it just happens.

Though I have written about writing, you know, God knows there's been a lot of that, I find the process as mysterious as I ever did, and I'm willing to leave it that way. I don't really see how this happens. It's nice that it does, and I hope it will continue.

EB   When did the idea for your seminars on writing, the theme "Write for Your Life" come to you? Of course the book and tape are now out of print and totally unavailable. And of course I haven't been able to lay hands on them.

LB   Well, I had already done a ton of writing about writing, because I started doing the *Writers Digest* column on the way back from the L.A. trip I was talking about. The summer of '76, I drove back east again from L.A.

I had sold an article written in the course of that trip to *Writers Digest*, and I made a point of stopping in Cincinnati on the way to New York, having lunch with them, and proposing a column to John Brady, who was then the editor of *WD*. They were responsive, and I did the column. Wound up doing it for the next fourteen years.

EB   Are you still writing for them?

LB   No. I had a disagreement with the magazine a couple of years ago, and the whole experience ended badly. They did not behave terribly well, actually. But it was good for me while it lasted, certainly, and it was interesting to do, you know. Sitting down once a month and writing a sort of open letter to the world about writing.

EB   How many columns did that amount to? That was quite a period of time.

LB It was, as I said, close to fourteen years. The first few months it was bimonthly. It was probably about 160 columns, something like that.

EB You have published four books about writing, including the manual for your seminars. How much of the material from *Writer's Digest* has been reprinted?

LB A fair amount. As much as needs to be, I suppose. There are quite a few columns in each book. I don't know what it comes to in chapters, but I think, probably, it must come close to a hundred of the columns. It is interesting how little duplication there was. When I edited the first collection, which was, as I said, probably about forty-eight columns, the only editing I did was combining two columns into one, because there was a similarity, and doing a little trimming here and there. There was one anecdote that was repeated in two columns.

EB Amazing.

LB Yeah.

EB You wouldn't think there would be that much to say about writing.

LB Well, I don't know if there is, actually. One of the problems I had with the magazine ultimately was that I didn't repeat myself enough. They felt that their readership had a lot of turnover, and they wanted to be able to address more fundamental points that I felt I'd already covered adequately and that didn't interest me enough to write about again.

But, anyway, the seminars. Lynne and I had taken some seminars in the New Age movement, I suppose you could call it. In particular, a seminar called "Loving Relationships Training," which was useful then. I don't know what the organization is like now. Most things like that deteriorate sooner or later, so I wouldn't be inclined to comment about it. I found the process very interesting. The structure of the seminar was such that I thought, gee, there'd probably be a way to put something together for writers, using this kind of process and this kind of technique, and it might be fun to do.

It seemed to me that most of the material designed to help writers addressed things that had already been done to death, or that were completely beside the point. They would bombard a person with data which nobody needed, whereas the relevant thing was the inner game of writing, which nobody seemed to address.

So I tried this idea out at a writers' conference in Indianapolis and it worked. It had an astonishing impact on people, and it was fun to do and it didn't seem to make any difference what level of writing proficiency anybody was at. In fact, you didn't have to know that when you were in the seminar.

EB What was the structure of the seminar? How did you go about it? I've never taken part in an encounter group or New Age seminar.

LB It's too complicated to explain. We self-published the book for the seminars. It's called *Write for Your Life*, and no, it's not available.

It's hard to explain, but there were a variety of interactional processes and automatic writing processes and things to stir one up and to address the beliefs one held that were inhibiting one as a writer, whatever. Anyway, I can't begin to explain it all, and I don't want to try and convey it here, but it was great fun for us. Lynne and I led the seminar all over the country, and we created a whole business to do this; organizers and ads and mailers—direct mail campaigns to enlist people.

There was no way to make any money at the damn thing, unfortunately, because, you know, we charged a hundred bucks for the seminar, and by the time we got done paying for the ads and the direct mail and the airlines and the hotel and this and that, we didn't make fifty cents an hour for our troubles. But we had a lot of fun and stretched ourselves in some interesting ways. It was good that way, and after we'd done it for about three years, it seemed to be taking an enormous amount of time. It took all my time. In fact, there was precious little writing that I did while we were involved in that.

EB How many would you do—say, one a month or more?

LB   No. We would do it in season. We would have one or two seasons a year, and for about three months we would do one seminar a week. But that's all we did. We were either running the seminar or on our way to it or on our way from it or doing the paperwork for it in the middle of the week. So it really took all our time.

EB   You held these all over the country?

LB   Yes. And after three years it was enough, you know. It wasn't something we wanted to do forever, anyway. And it got to feel increasingly like performance. I would be telling stories and I'd feel like an actor in a long run of a show, and I didn't want to do that. But I never do a signing or a show that somebody doesn't come up and say, "I took your seminar at Someplaceorother." So that's fine.

EB   Apparently, they were quite popular. You never had any trouble booking the seminars?

LB   Oh, yeah. We had trouble enrolling. Sure. It's a struggle, you know, with something like that. Sometimes we would only get twenty people and we wouldn't cover expenses. On the other hand, we couldn't get *too* many. It wasn't like a lecture. We couldn't work in a room with much more than eighty people.

EB   Not like those "How to Make a Killing in Real Estate" things?

LB   No, and we didn't have a big collection of tapes to sell afterwards. There was no way to exploit it. We just had the book.

EB   In a *Publishers' Weekly* interview you did a few years ago, you talked about the fact that you were quite happy with your life at that point. Your personal life had stabilized, you were having a lot of critical success with your books, and you were getting a lot of writing done. My guess is that since then that pattern has pretty much stayed the same. One of the things that seems important to your relationship is the trips you take. You've done some traveling overseas.

LB Quite a bit. Soon after Lynne and I were married we decided to put together a list of the places we'd like to go sometime or other, and ten minutes into this process we realized the pointlessness of it because we were just listing every place we'd ever been. We both have an appetite for travel. That may have gotten seriously impaired by a trip we took last summer to Sinkiang Province in northwestern China, which was such a difficult, arduous trip that it undercut our enthusiasm for that sort of thing. It slowed us down. We haven't rushed to go any place since then, because we came back from that trip just beat to hell.

EB Where are some of the places you've gone?

LB Well, we went to four countries in West Africa in '87. That was a wonderful experience. That was a terrific trip. That was under the auspices of the Institute for the Study of Noetic Sciences, which is the organization that Edgar Mitchell founded when he came back from the moon and decided that the interface between hard science and the psychic sciences was something he wanted to address. And this was a trip that went to—it focused on traditional medicine and shamanic healers in West Africa. So, in fact, there's a story in the new collection (*Some Days You Get the Bear*), called "Hillard's Ceremony," which grew right out of that. Most of my novels, as I said, are set in New York and are only pollinated by my travels, but my short stories are set all over the place and are often influenced by my travels.

Another trip that was very exciting—something of a stretch—was the one we did during the summer of '91. Lynne and I flew to Toulouse in the south of France and walked over the Pyrenees and across Spain on the Way of St. James—all the way across to Santiago de Compostela.

EB Quite a trip to do on foot. The only reason I know anything about that famous pilgrimage route is that the University of New Mexico Press published a beautiful picture book on the subject. You did the pilgrimage on your own? It wasn't part of a tour?

LB No, no. We just did it on our own.

EB   What gave you the idea? Why the pilgrimage of Santiago?

LB   Somebody told us about a friend of his who had done the trip. It was Jack Hitt, the fellow who put together the collaboration *The Perfect Murder*, which I contributed to. He had done it about ten years previously, and as soon as we heard about the walk we wanted to do it. There are guide books, but you just walk, you know.

EB   You've got to know where you're going.

LB   Yeah, yeah. Maps. And there are books that talk about the traditional route, but we didn't start out following the traditional route because we decided we'd just like to cross the Pyrenees and go through Andorra and around through Catalonia. So we took the longer route. As best I can calculate, we walked about 670 miles.

EB   In what period of time?

LB   About two and a half months. Typically, we would walk ten or fifteen miles a day.

EB   Sounds like a lot of fun, though.

LB   It would have been more fun if the packs had been lighter.

EB   You weren't camping, were you?

LB   No, but we had to carry sleeping bags, because they had a system of *refugios* for pilgrims along the route, which are free and which sometimes are the only game in town—in the area, but they don't have much in the way of comforts. They have very basic facilities, generally, and no blankets, so you would need a sleeping bag for those stops. And we would find that we could stay in *refugios* two or three nights in a row, and then we really wanted to be in a *hostal* of some sort, where there was hot water and such.

But you wouldn't have wanted to do it without sleeping bags, because there were enough times when you needed them, so you had to carry those and necessities, and the pack ended up pretty heavy. Even though we didn't have much in the way of clothes, the packs were pretty heavy. If I do it again, I'll carry less, and I may do it again.

EB Really? I would think it would be unlikely for you to repeat a trip, since there are so many places you haven't seen and things you haven't done.

LB Yeah. I wouldn't mind doing it. I might want to do it again. It's kind of special. It's not that I'm reluctant to explain the trip. It's that I find it difficult to do. I tried to write about it afterward for the *Times* travel section, and I had a lot of trouble with the writing. When I finished it, they weren't happy with the piece and wanted me to revise it, and I decided I'd rather kill it than revise it, because I couldn't make a travel piece out of it. It wasn't that kind of a thing—it was far more. But rather, I suppose, an inward journey, and even that was largely unconscious. It was kind of a test, you know. There was a definite ordeal aspect to it. I think we liked that part, too.

EB Along the lines of "something that doesn't have to be worked for isn't really worth as much," that a difficult experience is richer?

LB It was also something so demanding that the whole day was taken up with the doing of it. So that there was a point, for example, where it ceased to be a trip—a journey—in that the road was where we lived. The same thing has happened to me as I've rambled around the country here. It took longer for Lynn than for me, but there came a point where that was an everyday reality. It wasn't that we were on our way from here to there and we lived somewhere else. We were here. Period, you know.

EB The quest tale is the oldest literary form. I mean, from *Gilgamesh* to *Don Quixote*, from *Huckleberry Finn* to *On the Road*. The quest, the journey narrative has become especially close to the American experience. You already said that that trip was in the nature of a pilgrimage.

LB Historically, it was the second or third most important destination of Christian pilgrims in the Middle Ages.

EB Of course, you don't have any Catholic connections whatsoever.

LB Well, Lynne grew up Catholic, but I ceased long ago to have any formal religious connection.

EB How did you find the people on a journey like that? I mean, were they pretty friendly?

LB We barely did. That's the thing. We met other pilgrims on the road, of course, of an evening, and we would encounter them briefly during the day, but you walk your own pace, so we were never really walking with anybody else. We were with each other.

While English is the closest thing to a universal language, no one in the towns in northern Spain speaks it, and no one spoke English where we were, and while my Spanish would work to cope with food and water and shelter, that was about it. I could read the Spanish newspaper, but I couldn't really have a conversation in any real sense with anybody. One almost could in Castile and León, but in the rest of the areas, the accents were so strong and so regional that even if my Spanish had been pretty good, I would have been slowed down. And as soon as I got used to the way they were talking in one place, we walked into a place where they were talking different. So the only people we really met tended to be in towns where we would meet other people who were on the same journey. But most of the time we spent with each other. We were together probably about twenty-three hours a day.

EB Was that part of the reason for the trip?

LB It wasn't a reason for the trip. But it was an extraordinary test of a relationship. I can't imagine spending that kind of time with any other human being that ever walked the earth. We get along well. It's a good thing we're capable of giving each other a tremendous amount of space.

We're also capable of spending a lot of time in close quarters without going nuts.

EB   That's, I think, the real meaning of the word *intimacy*. I think most people take it on a physical level, and, really, that's the easy part. It's the other level that counts; that's more interesting.

LB   We had a wonderful time, and then, I think, any strong experience changes you. I'm sure that trip did in some way, though I can't point to anything. But I'm very, very glad we did it.

EB   Sounds like a lot of fun. Are the trips developing into an annual thing?

LB   Not exactly. Just when we get to it. It seems to me that I haven't really traveled that much when I look at all the places we haven't been.

EB   Are you traveling more now just because you have the economic freedom, or has something happened to encourage you?

LB   I don't know why I didn't travel a lot more earlier. Fear, I guess. For the longest time I was convinced that I would have no end of difficulties if I went someplace where they didn't speak English. That turned out to be very easy. And I traveled in the sixties and early seventies. I went to Ireland a lot.

EB   What was your connection to Ireland?

LB   I don't know. My feeling is that there's a strong past-life connection there. I was drawn when I was a little kid to Irish music and just always had a feel for the place, and that is the first place out of the country that I ever went. In '64 I guess. I went there and felt immediately at home and went back there almost every year after that for the next several years. I think the most time I ever spent there was two months. But I haven't been there since '74. Lynne and I were going to go this year and changed our minds. I think we'll just drive around northern New England.

EB What happened on the China trip?

LB It was just a very difficult trip under very primitive conditions. It is known to be the worst desert in the world, the Taklamakan, and it was exhausting.

EB Why did you go?

LB Well, it's a place nobody's been. I mean, really, nobody's been there. We were the first Americans on that stretch of the southern Silk Road— ever. We were only the second or third group of Westerners in that part of the country since Marco Polo. The trip was listed in the catalogue of the company that we traveled with before, and we thought, Gotta do it.

EB Go for it.

LB Yeah. Beat the shit out of us.

EB Did you walk it?

LB Nah, nah. There was a stretch on camel, but outside of that it was in overland vehicles. But traveling on things that you couldn't call a road. Putting the best possible light on it, you couldn't call it a road, and it was very difficult traveling. I'm not sorry we went, but it still hasn't been a long enough time for me to remember the experience fondly. Memory, fortunately, improves almost everything, otherwise we all would have long since killed ourselves.

EB If you hadn't been pretty seasoned travelers, it probably would have been worse, don't you think?

LB It couldn't have been much worse. If it had been any worse, we would have killed our guides and left.

EB Besides going around New England by car, what else have you got lined up?

LB I don't know. As I said, this trip to New England—we were originally going to go to Turkey this June and then we decided, no, let's do something easier. Let's just go to Ireland and rent a car for about two weeks, and then we decided, the hell with that. Let's just go driving around New England, New Hampshire, Vermont for ten days or two weeks. And by the time we get around to it, we may scale it back further and just go to the Bronx Zoo for an hour and a half.

EB On the home front, you've recently bought an apartment. I gather you're pretty much settled into New York, the Village?

LB That was decided when we moved back from Florida. By the end of the two-year trip around the country, we had become very clear on where we wanted to live. We drove around with the thought that maybe we wanted to come back to New York and maybe we didn't, and we were open to the idea of finding someplace that we liked better. And we realized that while there were quite a few places that were much better by any objective standard, it didn't matter. We realized that it was beside the point and that New York was home to us in ways that no other place could possibly be.

If we were twenty years old, we might want to move someplace else and start afresh, but we had already created a whole life here that we were attached to—places and people—in ways that we couldn't hope to replace elsewhere. We knew that wherever we went, in no time at all we would just miss New York.

So we moved back here and really got to fall in love with the city all over again. Although I must say we were never away from it for a substantial period of time. When we were living in Florida we were probably back here three or four times a year. We were frequently coming for a greater or lesser period of time.

I'm very glad to be in the city. The Village is the part of the city that I've spent the most time in and am most attached to, and we were right where we wanted to be in it. So geographically, I'm very happy with where I am. When I had my first co-op job in New York in the summer of '56, I lived in the Village, and the first place we lived was a furnished room.

There were three of us, and we had this large furnished room about four flights up on West Fourteenth Street, just about a block from where Lynne and I are living now. That's how far I've come in thirty-seven years.

EB A block.

LB Yeah. About a step a year.

EB What about the supposed deterioration of the city? Your own character, Scudder, comments often on the element of random violence, for example. You don't feel that in your Golden Years, so to speak, you need to have a calmer environment?

LB No, not really. The faults that Scudder sees in the city, I think, are not so much specific to the city as they are universal these days. I think the whole country and the whole world is like that.

EB The twentieth century ending in a kind of millennial madness?

LB Yeah. I've done a little reading the past couple of years on New York City history, which I didn't know a whole lot about. I still don't know a whole lot about it, but I know a little more than I did, and it's always been like this.

And at various times in history, it's been worse than this. I know there's a point in one of the Scudder novels where he's reading something from criminal history in England in the eighteenth century and he's both reassured and depressed by a similar observation that it was always thus. On the one hand, it's nice to know it's not getting any worse. On the other hand, it's disheartening to know this seems to be the human condition.

So that doesn't bother me. In a lot of ways, I think this is probably as good a place to grow old as there is.

EB For a country boy like myself, New York is pretty overwhelming. The entire population of the town I live in would fit in the apartment complex we're sitting in at the moment. The entire city of Gallup could move in tomorrow. And there are bigger ones, you know, much bigger ones. On my last trip here someone pointed out a skyscraper and said, "That build-ing has its own zip code." I was impressed. It turns out that there are two dozen or so buildings like that. Everything here is on such a scale.

LB There are a lot of interesting things about the city. The city popula-tion now is, right now, just about 50 percent foreign born, and that was true a hundred years ago. Yet it was not true fifty years ago. There's been a great increase in immigration into the city, though it's always been a port of entry and it's always had a high immigrant population. It's in-creased recently. And the Asianization of New York has been remarkable.

EB What are the specific characteristics of the city that appeal to you?

LB Well, at this point it's hard to tell, because it's home, and how do you factor that into the equation? But there are a couple of things I always think of. The energy of New York, certainly. The pace, the speed. When I was living in Fort Myers, I remember, I went into the drugstore there once to buy a newspaper. It was fifty cents and I had fifty cents in change. And there was this lethargic line there, going nowhere fast. So I went up and I put fifty cents on the counter for the paper and walked on. Well, that's what you do here. And the clerk there, who was not in any hurry for any-thing to happen, let me assure you, said, "What's the matter? You in a rush?" And I said, "Yeah." She was very offended, as though I had in-sulted her. Well, I'd saved all of us time, herself included, you know, and I thought, How can they not get that down here?

And I was in La Guardia Airport not too long after that—there's a cafe-teria there, and there was a sign that said, "It is not impolite to pass people who are waiting for something." I thought, that sign is for people from out of town, because everybody here knows that. I like that kind of energy. I remember Reggie Jackson, talking about New York, said, "You tell a New Yorker the first line and he's got the whole page."

I like that I don't have to have a car. I like that the whole city is easily accessible to me, either by public transportation or by walking around. I like that I can live on the street.

In other cities, you know, you're a writer and you're in your car all the time and you're not being fed by the city. Here, I am. On every walk there's something. Every time I go out to buy a paper there's people around. There's life happening. It's very easy for me to be constantly soaking up things, some of which ultimately wind up between book covers. Transmuted a whole lot. But when you write a lot of books, you certainly run out of whatever you were originally drawing upon. There has to be some kind of continuing input. If the input is from other books, there's something wrong with that. Then you're just reworking other people's material.

So I like that about this city. I must say, I like most places that I go to, so it's not that this is the only place I can stand. I enjoy the people, the pace, and everything else most places I go to. But this place makes sense.

EB Most New Yorkers I have known, even transplanted ones, have a certain arrogance about them. New Yorkers believe they live in God's country and everybody else just lives. Other people just survive. New York is where everything of value is. They have the lock on reality.

LB It's very parochial in that respect. I know lots of New Yorkers who think that this is the whole country and that nobody else is out there, except for occasionally somebody plowing a field. They don't get that. And that's a failing of vision which I find amusing. But given that you've got to live someplace, this is the place I'd pick.

EB It feeds your inner self.

LB Absolutely, absolutely. When I was living in Fort Myers, I was thinking, If I'm going to live here forever—and at that point I still thought I was—if I'm going to live here, I should eventually set some of my stuff here. My writing.

EB It worked well for Travis McGee.

LB I thought, It's not categorically less interesting than other places that way, and a novel can be set anyplace. Will I set things here? And I thought, I probably won't, because I don't know what lives are like here. In the intuitive way that you know. I mean, people in New York don't rush up to me to tell me their secrets. There's an intuitive sense I have of what they're like here in New York, and I didn't have it there.

Key West, I might have. That's in Florida, too, but it's similar in some way to where I live in New York, so that I had some sense of people there. So if I had lived in Key West, I might have written things set there. But I couldn't use the people in Fort Myers. I didn't get them. I didn't crack the code.

EB I wonder sometimes if we aren't predisposed to certain places. I've lived most of my adult life in Gallup, and I feel about the Southwest the way you feel about New York, even though I travel around a great deal and like other parts of the country. I seem to be tuned into that place the way you are here. I know what's happening. I know what to do in a given situation. I'm happy in an Indian bar where other Anglos would be terrified, or at least extremely uneasy. I know exactly what's going to happen.

LB The writer that I am fondest of and whom I still reread is John O'Hara. I've reread all of his work innumerable times. So I get a lot out of that.

EB For people who haven't read O'Hara, what do you think is his strength?

LB Well, he wrote wonderfully, and I always found it very easy to enter into and believe his books, and his characters had lives that seemed to me to be real lives.

EB O'Hara's people often seemed to me rather tragic. Am I misremembering him?

LB No. Everything real is tragic. No one gets out of this alive, you know.

EB But isn't he a bit more of a fatalist than average?

LB Maybe. I just ultimately know that I found his novels believable in terms of the nature of human lives, the way the evolution of human relationships are. It's possible there's less there than meets my eye, you know.

EB I wasn't fishing for that, I want to know what it is that you are responding to in his work.

LB Well, I don't know.

EB He was certainly successful.

LB Enormously successful. I don't know whether his work will endure or not. But I don't know what that means.

EB Do you worry about that personally?

LB Yes. I suppose there's a point in one's life where one is more inclined to. But I look at writers who are or are not read fifty years after their death and I'll be damned if I can see what makes that happen.

EB There's no logic to it to me.

LB Yeah. Not only is there no logic to it, but if there's no afterlife at all, it can't matter. If there is, I have to assume that any afterlife worth the afterliving would consist of one caring about things other than what a bunch of clowns are or are not reading down on this planet.

Why would you give a shit? Either you move on to something else or you're in hell. So, I don't know. It's hard to know what one writes for, actually. There's that line of Johnson's, that "no man but a blockhead wrote but for money," though I'm not sure exactly what he meant. I don't know if that's as crass and cynical as it sounds in the quoting. I think he may have meant that anyone who wrote with the expectation of much more than that was nuts. And that way, it makes sense to me, you know.

EB I hope he was being facetious.

LB I don't think there's much else you can expect, except whatever the reward is. I know I write in the hope of getting it right. You don't have to have done this for too long before the reviews only matter in the sense that they will or will not affect sales. You're crazy if you look to critics for validation. If you can get their applause, that only means that you can get deflated by their disapproval, and what's the point of that?

EB What is validation? A thousand dollars a copy for your first novel on the rare book market?

LB No. I don't know what it is. It's gratifying, certainly, to see sales increase. I like that.

EB Not just for the money.

LB No, certainly not just for the money. Because for all that we see the advances people like Stephen King and Mary Clark get, that's not a legitimate reason to want to write. I guess there are people now who are misguided enough to go into writing because they fantasize about rich rewards from it. But most writers struggle and work very hard to make a pretty bad living.

In recent years I've been fortunate. I've been doing reasonably well, which is certainly very nice, and I prefer it to not doing well. But I've reached a fairly high standing in my profession, and if I'd reached the same level in real estate or investment banking or insurance or almost *anything* else, I would be a multimillionaire, I think. I would have a lot of dough and would have had it a lot earlier. But writing isn't lucrative compared to anything else.

The reward is twofold—satisfaction as an artist and the satisfaction of selling more copies. One is the ego, which just always wants more— "Give me, give me," you know. "Make me feel important." There's a certain amount of that. A more worthy thing, or more estimable, I suppose, is that I really like being read. I don't begrudge the copies that go to the libraries and that circulate among readers—that's fine.

I really like the idea of my work being read. Ultimately, the work is the important thing if you stay with it for any length of time. It must be that way, because the money, whether you make it or not, you don't keep it, you don't take it with you—it doesn't change your life.

The work, finally, is it. For all its frustrations, for all that you never get it quite right. Evan Hunter was saying the other day, he spent however many years, forty years, whatever, trying to write a perfect book. It never quite comes out perfect.

EB Among current mystery writers, who do you think comes the closest?

LB I tend not to want to respond to that because I don't want to say anything favorable or unfavorable about living writers. I don't want to leave people out. I don't want to condemn anyone, even through omission. I think there's an awful lot of good work being done.

Also, I'm probably not the person to ask, because I don't read as much anymore and I don't finish very much of what I start. Somewhere around age thirty-five, I realized that simply because I started reading a book did not mean I had to finish it. Many people seem to find that out about that age. Have you noticed that?

EB I came to the same conclusion, as most serious readers do.

LB Before that I compulsively finished every book I started. Then I realized that life was too short and life's books were too long and to hell with it. And now, even books that I enjoy, more often than not, I put down a third or half way in and find I'm not inclined to pick them up again. And, of course, with the great majority, I read two pages of them and I can't go on.

One of the plusses or minuses of having enough of a body of published work is that publishers send you books for quotes they can use in the jacket copy. And either they don't send you anything or you get three books a week and the galleys just rain in. I'm the worst person in the world to send a private-eye novel to in the expectation that I'll love it, because it's almost certain that I won't. I've read too many. I write them myself. I don't want this voice drumming in my ear, you know.

EB At the moment there's a tremendous upswing, renewed interest, whatever, in detective fiction. That was one of the things addressed at the Key West seminar we were both at. And the consensus there among the writers was that the structure of the murder mystery imposes order on a disorderly world. The detective somehow makes things come out right and sees that justice is served in an unjust world, and that seemed to be the central reason for the popularity of genre. I'm not so sure that I agree.

LB I'm not sure I agree, either. I think that has been an element. I know one woman—an extremely omnivorous reader—and the book she reads every night when she's going to sleep must be a mystery because she can only really relax with something where she knows it will all be worked out in the end. That's one person, you know, but it's an interesting example in aid of the first theory.

I think there are a couple of explanations. One, I think crime fiction was always enormously popular, but there was a tendency to hide the fact. As soon as a book had any pretension, any chance of strong commercial success, the publisher tried to conceal that it was a mystery and called it something else.

That really didn't break down until Christie's two posthumous novels hit the best-seller list and it was just unmistakable that they were mysteries and undeniable that they were best sellers, so what the hell, you know? That began to change publishers' attitudes and the marketplace's view of things.

Another thing right now is that there is a very real correlation between the improved status of the mystery and the improved readership of the mystery and the phenomenal growth of interest in nonfiction. True crime books sell at levels they never used to before. Now you can't go in a grocery store without some son-of-a-bitch writing a book about the latest serial killer, or whatever.

EB They had book deals going on the Waco, Texas, thing before it even ended.

LB I don't know what the social reason for this is, but it's clear that there is a preoccupation with crime to a greater extent than in the past, and that has something to do with the popularity of the books. I think that the pernicious anemia in much modern literary fiction has something to do with it.

EB Mysteries get more popular as so-called mainstream fiction gets more inaccessible?

LB Exactly. More inaccessible and less story.

EB Mysteries still have a plot and characters.

LB Right. And then, also, there's "magical realism," which has a following, but it's not a universal following. People who really want things to make literal sense are not going to be happy with those books. So if you want to find something with a story in it and characters in it, you may have to look for it in the mystery genre.

I did a piece in *American Heritage* that's a sort of personal overview of mystery fiction. I had an article in *American Heritage* a couple of years ago about our quest for cities named Buffalo, and I got to know the editor and he asked me to do a piece on crime fiction. Specifically American crime fiction, it being *American Heritage.*

I did that and a top-ten list of my all-time favorites. Actually, it's sixteen favorites. I couldn't limit it to ten. All men. That will piss people off.

I was limiting myself to dead writers, and there aren't that many deceased female writers that are deserving. The only one I could think of that I might almost have included was Craig Rice, but in the end I didn't include her. The other women writers who certainly would have made the list otherwise were Sayers and Christie, and they're both British. Anyway, this was very much a personal list, and those were the guys who were on it.

EB You didn't consider including living writers?

LB No, not really. I'm fond of a great many, and my approval or lack thereof has nothing to do with their merit.

EB For many years I have been both fascinated and infuriated by the fact that a lot of first-rate American writers have been critically and commercially neglected because they chose to write about the American West. Not the Western writers, like L'Amour, but serious novelists like Vardis Fisher and H. L. Davis (who won a Pulitzer). Mystery writers seem to suffer from an even greater stigma. A relatively small group of eastern literati get to decide who gets published and who gets appreciated.

LB Sure. The mystery genre has not been taken seriously. Has not been considered serious literature. And you could certainly argue that a novel that has the solution of an intricate puzzle as the main thrust of the book doesn't really clamor to be taken seriously. It's entertainment.

I wonder, sometimes, if it matters. Critical reputation and the enthusiasm of actual readers are clearly two different things, which don't often overlap that much, anyway. If I had to have one or the other, I'd certainly rather have the enthusiasm of the readers. One thing that makes me realize how fortunate writers are is when I look at friends of mine who are graphic artists—visual artists—and the difference in the nature of their business and mine is towering.

What I depend on, ultimately, for a living, is the approbation of people who buy the book in hard cover for twenty bucks or in paperback for five and read it, and they buy it because they want to read it.

I have a friend who paints. His canvases sell for ten to twenty thousand dollars. Some. Not often. But that's what his price is.

Nobody pays that because they think this would look nice over the sofa. They pay it because a gallery manages to convince them that this would be important to include in their collection or because some museum feels that it is necessary to have this in its collection. There's no relationship, really, between what he's doing and somebody who looks at it and is or is not moved by it. I'm glad the writing world is not like that. I think that's awful.

EB I'm sure most artists do too. I think illustrators are lucky in that respect.

LB Illustrators are very lucky in that respect, and people who are doing popular art of any sort are lucky in that respect. At least there's a real relationship between what they are doing and their audience—who is looking at it.

EB Weirdly enough, I first read Lawrence Block because of Robert McGinnis.

LB The cover artist.

EB I have a real thing about McGinnis covers, which might have something to do with why publishers used him so much.

LB I don't know anything about cover art. What did he do?

EB All the Tanners. All the Tanners are McGinnis covers.

LB Are they really?

EB Yeah. I even bought multiple copies of them because of the covers, believe it or not.

LB I'm sure he didn't do the first one, *The Thief Who Couldn't Sleep,* because that's utterly different and it's a lousy cover.

EB I've never had the original paperback of that one.

LB So that's who did those? McGinnis?

EB He's wonderful. But most people wouldn't know him by name.

LB Yeah. But they were my books, for Christ sake. I could have paid some attention to who did it.

EB I read the M. E. Chaber series, Carter Brown, lots of others because of those covers. Some of them probably didn't deserve to be read at all. Being frugal, I read the books, even though I bought them for the cover paintings. That was how I first discovered you.

LB There's a story about a guy who was doing cover paintings for Fawcett—for Westerns. An editor at Fawcett was very sorry he had to turn down a couple of paintings that the guy had brought him and discovered that the fellow didn't seem at all dismayed.

He found out later, you know, they were paying something like seven fifty or a thousand dollars for the cover art, and after they paid him, whether they used them or not, the guy took them all down to this gallery in Dallas and was selling them for fifteen thousand dollars a painting. So he didn't even care whether they used them or not.

EB Frank McCarthy came to fame and fortune via cover art for paperback Westerns. My favorite is a largely forgotten artist named A. Leslie Ross. He did hundreds and hundreds of covers for pulps, and he did most of the early Popular Library Westerns, and he's not listed in a single art reference I can find.

EB Speaking of collectible paperbacks and collecting in general, some of your books are quite elusive.

LB I don't know much about the collecting market. I know that there are some books that it seems to me are brought to me rather infrequently at shows. Books that I just don't see very often.

EB Which, presumably, are scarce and therefore collectible.

LB I would think so.

EB I tried to put together—and read—a full run of your books in preparation for this interview, and I discovered some interesting things. Of the Bernie Rhodenbarr books, *Burglar in the Closet* is the hardest one to find, and there's no particular reason for it that I can see. Usually the first book in a series is the toughest to find.

LB *Choosers* should be tougher. One reason it might not be, it occurs to me, is that I got those thousand copies of *Burglars Can't Be Choosers* into the collector market. Otherwise, they would have been remaindered and most of them would have been pulped, one way or another. I may have increased the number of available firsts that way. I don't know.

EB It's also interesting that with very few exceptions, paperback originals just never really get that collector frenzy. There are only a few exceptions.

LB No. They're collected by paperback collectors.

EB Jim Thompson is one of the pricey exceptions. There's no other publication of most of his books. David Goodis, Charles Williford, and the early John D. MacDonald. And *Junkie,* of course.

LB I've seen Tanner firsts going for twenty-five, thirty dollars. That's—

EB Probably not realistic, though. I mean, they're around.

LB Are they?

EB Of course, in the collectible market, as you must know, condition is everything, and finding great copies is a whole other thing. Not many paperbacks survive "as new." What collectors want is the unread one, and, of course, they're not going to take it home then and read it.

LB Well, no. I wouldn't either if I paid fifty bucks for it because it was pristine. It makes much more sense to do my reading in a copy I got for five bucks because the cover was gone or something.

LB I recently had someone came up at a signing with a copy of *Mona* that was absolutely new.

EB The collector's dream.

LB The kind that when you autograph it you want to open the cover very carefully.

EB I saw a guy practically faint once. He handed a copy like that to an author at a signing and the author flipped the cover back and pressed it down with the heel of his hand and the fan just freaked out. He took it back. He wouldn't even let the guy sign it after that.

LB It's surprising that the writer wouldn't know better than to do that. I was at a store one time signing stock someplace and the owner was opening the books for me like that. It was his store, so I wasn't going to say anything, but I was astonished.

EB The collecting craze is causing some interesting behavior by fans at signings these days, like having them ask you to backdate your signature to the date of publication, or put in generic inscriptions, or draw something, or put in long quotes. Especially asking for a fake date or place of inscription.

LB No. I haven't been asked to do that.

EB That's a common one now. Last year I was at the Poisoned Pen in Phoenix with Walter Satterthwait, and some guy came up with an armful of books and he had long passages copied out of them that he wanted Walter to write in as part of his inscription.

LB I had a guy who came up and he would find some line from the book that he wanted me to write on the fly leaf or the title page, whatever, and sign. I had no objection to that. It showed me he had a more-than-passing interest in the material, which was nice. At least he had to read it to find the passages to quote. So I didn't mind that. Long passages, I don't know.

EB Quite lengthy. Of course, I think that Walter's response was based on the fact that the guy didn't want the books inscribed to him. He just wanted the quotation written in there and then signed. It seemed obvious he wanted something he could resell profitably.

LB I don't have a lot of objections to people not wanting the books signed to them because, to acknowledge the realities of the marketplace, personal inscriptions devalue a collectible book, unless the signee is famous himself.

EB That's right.

LB I don't have a problem with that. I have a problem with the guy who comes up with a sack of twenty remaindered copies of the same title and wants them all signed. I just tell him to go to hell, you know. There used to be a guy in the field who did that. It was this guy's boast that he never bought a book in a store and this was to finance his kids' college or something. Well, I don't think it's that important to me that his kids go to college.

EB Exactly. He could at least be nice about it.

LB It doesn't matter that much to me personally. I'm in the store for two hours, what do I care where the books came from? But the store sponsoring the signing should get to sell a book now and then. I don't object to people coming with a batch, though I'll try to say, "I'll do three; then you can go to the back of the line."

Most writers will do that now because there are other people there and they just came with one book and they shouldn't have to wait six weeks to get it signed. But I don't mind doing it unless I'm starting to get tired.

EB Do you always chat with the people in line or does that just sort of depend on how they relate to you?

LB Up to a point. You know, you have the feeling you want to be friendly. I like doing signings. I really enjoy it. When Morrow sends me on a tour, I wish they'd send me not to seventeen cities, but to fifty. I really enjoy it. I like travel anyway, and I like meeting people. I greatly enjoy meeting booksellers. The last tour I was on was bookstore intensive. I went to something like 250 stores in three weeks. Mostly just signing store stock. There weren't that many formal signings, but a ton of drop-ins and shmoozing with the booksellers and signing store copies of my books, and I enjoy all of that.

And as far as conversations with people on line, the difficult thing is that you get the same six questions a hundred times and you don't want to give people short shrift, but at the same time it's very difficult to pretend this is the first time anybody asked me if I was going to write another book about Bernie or Scudder, whatever the hell it is.

It's also a trial when the questions are witless. But, again, it's part of the game, and people shouldn't have had to pass some test in order to be on line. It's gratifying that they want to come at all.

EB I'm a believer. I really am. I've been on all three sides of the table—bookseller, author, and fan, and I'm a believer. I think that there are careers that have been significantly enhanced by cooperative authors who may speed up the process of discovery by winning over fans and book dealers.

LB Maybe. But the most salient factor is that I do enjoy doing it, and when the time comes that I don't, I suspect that I'll stop. But so far, I'm enjoying it.

However, what I was getting at is you sometimes get the feeling that there are people who are there and—I don't know what it is that they want from me, but I have a feeling that they want something from me that I don't have to give.

EB A little sympathetic magic. That meeting you will make them smarter or more beautiful. That you're somebody whose touch cures warts.

LB Something. I don't know what it is. Sometimes it's clear to me that they wanted something from me and I didn't supply it. I don't know what it was. And there are people who want some kind of personal relationship and I can't have that. "Could we have dinner after this?" Well, no. It's a long tour, and when I'm done at the end of the day, I don't even want to go to dinner with the store owner. I want to go sit in front of the TV and eat something that the hotel sent up from room service. Because it's tiring and as enjoyable as it is, there's an energy drain in the situations.

EB There are individual stores now—some of the specialty mystery stores and a few catalog dealers—that are having an impact on the business. Dealers who can actually influence an author's sales to some extent. At a signing they can move four or five hundred copies of an author that they like. Book Carnival in Orange [California] sold more than fifteen hundred of Dean Koontz's last book. I mean, they really have a following, and they have a big turnout for their signings. And when they begin to promote somebody, their influence can be felt. Having the goodwill of booksellers certainly doesn't hurt.

LB I think it's important. I think it's still a business where hand selling is important. I don't know that that generates best-seller-list numbers, though.

EB Maybe not.

LB But I think that I, as a writer, like to form a relationship with a bookseller, however—oh, however rudimentary it is, even if it's just a hello and a handshake and a half a dozen sentences. But that does me some good. I think so. I think you form a relationship with the readers, whether it's through a meeting or through their responding to something in the book that makes them inclined to want to read the next book.

EB Of course that needs to be there too.

LB Sure. That absolutely has to be there, or you can forget it.

EB Last year at the meeting of Left Coast Crime in Anaheim, I observed something interesting. That's a good fan organization, by the way. They really draw a good crowd. Everything's been so well organized, especially the two that were held in San Francisco. They had a nice hospitality room set up, and there was quite a group gathered. They were obviously old hands and acquainted with one another, and they were talking about having gone to Bouchercon the year that Tony Hillerman was the featured speaker and gave a talk on inept criminals and wonderfully bungled crimes.

The group got quite animated at that point, and I was really impressed by their enthusiasm. It was like it was an unforgettable moment—a high spot.

Obviously, that helped Hillerman's career. There had to be hundreds of people in the audience who hadn't read him yet who were so impressed, amused, and entertained, hearing him tell these funny crime stories, that they ran out and bought his books. The enthusiasm in that group was wonderful and each one would throw in a "Yeah. He's sure a good sport," and "I always love it when he shows up," and so on and so forth. There was that tremendous sense of goodwill.

LB It's important to a degree, but an essential thing to remember is that will get a person to buy *one* book.

EB Well, you know, the rest is up to the author.

LB Absolutely, absolutely.

EB But somehow you have to get that first book into the reader's hands. There is a tremendous element of luck here, of course. And the publisher has a lot to do with a writer's success often. I have a friend with four books who just doesn't have a career going, and I think the books are very good. A couple of them are *very* good. Partly the problem is in just not reaching the public, rather than not pleasing readers once you reach them.

LB It may take a long time to have some success. For a lot of us it takes a long time.

EB   But then a book like *Horse Latitudes* [by Robert Ferrigno] comes along and it gets rave reviews in half the publications in America, though I thought it was just an ordinary book. If I didn't know better I'd think a bunch of reviewers around the country got together at a convention and said, "Let's play a practical joke on the mystery readers this year. We'll put a copy of this book in every bookcase in the country." Like the fraternity back East years ago who tried to get a chimpanzee graduated by taking classes for him. The second book, *Cheshire Moon*, is really good, however.

LB   No, no. The publisher may have been very successful in attracting critical attention. Also the book may have been what Hollywood has chosen to call *high concept*, and that makes an enormous difference. Several new writers of limited skill and storytelling ability are hitting the bestseller list regularly and what their books have is that there's a strong commercial premise.

EB   The first time I ever heard the term *high concept* I asked what it meant, though it does rather define itself. My friend Ray Ring said, "What that means in Hollywood is you can tell it and sell it in a single sentence."

LB   What it means is that you can get the point across in one sentence and it's so simple that even a studio executive can understand what you're saying. That's absolutely what it is, and there are a lot of worthy books of which that is not true.

You can say it in one sentence and there's something arresting about the sentence that finishes it. I mean, there are lots of my books where you can get across what it is in one sentence, but so what? But there are lots of perfectly worthy books where one sentence isn't going to make you say, "Oh, wow, there could be a movie in that" or "Let's see how that works." Something can be high concept and it can be wonderful, or it can be high concept and there's still nothing there.

EB   I still believe in publicity, doing the shows and doing the signings, being nice to the booksellers, being nice to the public, especially in those early stages. Though I know a couple of authors who should probably stay home because they just turn people off.

LB I know a few of those. Good writers, but they just can't deal with the public. They're just no good at it. That's very true, and that doesn't get mentioned as much. Barbara Mertz said in an interview in *Mystery Scene* that she thinks it's terrible that publishers make people go out on the road, and she doesn't think it's important and doesn't think it does any good and can point to a lot of writers who never leave the house and they sell better than the ones who are out there. I don't think a person's well advised to do it unless they truly enjoy it.

EB I've seen Mary Higgins Clark two or three times, and she is so engaging.

LB She's wonderful.

EB She is unusually well spoken; quick, witty, smart, and hilariously funny. She presents herself well, and she's extremely funny in person. But I've tried to read her books and they just don't speak to me.

LB I must have heard her basic talk, "How I became a writer"—I must have heard that ten times over the years. And you know, I'm never bored. She's a wonderful speaker. She could host a talk show. And she does herself enormous good, but she enjoys doing that and she's a trooper—a pro. She can tell the same anecdote everyday for two weeks running and it doesn't bore.

EB The character of Scudder is the creation of a writer in mid-career. A writer who has gotten past feeling around for narrative voice. Who is comfortable with the kind of material he wants to write, the effects he wants to achieve, the philosophical viewpoint he espouses. Scudder is as mature—weighty but not really world-weary—as Chip Harrison and Evan Tanner were youthful good fun. And right this minute, he's one of the most fascinating detectives in crime fiction. Certainly, one of the most popular.

But as a person he seems to have deliberately set up a life that most people would consider fairly minimal. He doesn't want responsibility. He doesn't want too much clutter, physical, emotional, or financial. He's really got the process of life down to just survival. And that hasn't changed much over the course of his literary career, though he has evolved, especially in getting sober. He's got life just about down to the minimum, and that's all he can handle. Can you recall what were you thinking when you created this particular character?

LB Well, I don't know. I don't know what I was thinking. It's hard enough to remember what I was thinking yesterday. I began developing this series toward the end of '73, and it's certainly no secret that there were parallels between my circumstances and the character's at the time.

I had separated from my first wife in July of '73 and had moved back to New York and was living in a studio apartment on West Fifty-eighth Street, and Scudder was living in a hotel on that same block and had, at an indeterminate point in time, separated from his wife and family and was living alone in the city.

Beyond that, the impulse, who knows? I do know that the Scudder books were conceived of as a series. At the time, my then-agent got in touch and said he felt that Dell would be very much interested in some sort of tough series to replace the Carter Brown books. Brown had either died or was getting toward the end of the trail, and my agent felt that Dell might be amenable to something and suggested I write a series about a tough cop.

And I thought about that, and it became clear to me that I would be more comfortable writing about a former cop than a current one; that I wasn't interested in police procedure nor would I ever be able to get that much into a character who was part of a bureaucracy.

So, probably as much for convenience as anything else, I put Scudder in the neighborhood that I was living in, because that was what I was seeing everyday. And the character evolved. He had what you might call a minimal life, but then I think that's what one does when one goes and takes a hotel room and is waiting for life to take a direction.

That's how the Matt Scudder series developed. I don't know quite what mid-career means. I like to think it's like middle-age, which is defined as that period in life which starts five years from however old you are now. I think probably mid-career is similar.

EB I meant it in the sense that for so many series characters—for most series characters—they began as the author's first creation. Some series characters mature and develop with their creators, but many don't, and they get stale or trite. Or the author has to abandon them because of faults he built into them before he knew better. Tony Hillerman abandoned Joe Leaphorn and then found a way to go back and pick him up again, with the help of the more youthful, flexible Jim Chee.

You had already evolved as a writer, so you could create a series protagonist who was mature, tough-minded, somewhat scarred, low-profile, and ultimately more interesting and more believable than the run-of-the-mill comic-book hero. As I recall, you had three Scudder books written before the first one was published, so you had some confidence in what actually was a fairly offbeat character.

LB Well, no. That isn't quite the case. The specific reason why there were three written before they were published is that the Scudder series was conceived of as a series and contracted for as a series. So I knew from the beginning that I was going to write three books, and I did.

EB You don't appear to have worried about whether the Scudder character was going to go over or not, in spite of having given him some rather peculiar affiliations and personality quirks.

LB I never really give that much of a shit about what people are going to like. I knew that the books would get published, and I knew if there was a way, I would write them the best I could. That's the only way I normally approach anything. But not in terms of whether or not the world is going to like this particular character.

EB   How do you feel about the values and attitudes he reflects about contemporary society?

LB   I don't really think of my books in those terms. I write intuitively, and I don't take that kind of an overview of them before, during, or after the writing of the book. I don't particularly pay attention to that kind of thing when reading other people, and I certainly don't with my own books.

EB   But you've created a popular series detective who has a decidedly loose interpretation of justice and morality. He doesn't think there's anything particularly wrong with bribes to policemen, for example. One of his best friends is a murderer. His girlfriend is a prostitute. All of that is a little unusual for the genre. The private eye has always been a sort of white knight with, traditionally, an almost simplistic black-and-white view of justice and morality—except maybe about matters of sex. And you have a guy who is almost on the other side but not in the sort of comic way that Bernie Rhodenbarr is. How deliberate were those things, those elements of his life?

LB   I already said I don't think in terms of what people are going to like or what a story should be. I just take what the story is and what the characters are and I let it happen on the page. To my mind, the worst way to write a book is to force it to be the way you decide it should be. I can't write that way.

Let me try it this way. I write books the way they make sense to me. You know the story about the moron who found the lost horse when no one else could, and they asked him how he did it and he said, "I asked myself, if I was a horse, where would I go?"

And that's how I write. The book has its own reality. The characters do what they have to do. And I'm not being ingenuous here and pretending that I don't make a great many decisions, but that's how I make those decisions.

EB   Ten or twelve years ago, you said in an interview that you probably weren't going to write about Scudder anymore, and then in the last three or four years he has been featured in some of your most powerful and best writing.

LB   Well, there have been several times where it seemed to me as though I was through with him. After *Eight Million Ways to Die*, where Scudder comes to terms with his alcoholism and goes through a catharsis there, it seemed to me as though it would be very difficult to do anything after that. Although each of the first five books is a novel, complete in itself, it seemed to me as though they constituted one five-volume novel, and that had come to an end, at the end of *Eight Million Ways to Die*. And I regretted this because I enjoyed the character. I enjoyed seeing the world through his eyes, and I enjoyed writing in that voice very, very much. I felt that, without question, the Scudder books were the best work I'd ever done.

So I didn't want to have to abandon that. I made several attempts at a sixth Scudder book that didn't work. I threw them all away after a greater or lesser amount of time. I think I wrote about 150 pages of one and stuck it in the incinerator and abandoned the others at different stages. Then I wrote *When the Sacred Ginmill Closes*. First I wrote it in the form of a short story, "By the Dawn's Early Light," and then I realized that it could be substantially expanded with the addition of a couple of other plot elements, and it became a novel.

That was the sixth book, and I know it's a lot of people's favorite because it's, oh, there's a word "painterly" that illustrators will use to describe a work that has moved more from an illustration toward fine art in some of its techniques. Similarly, in certain ways, *When the Sacred Ginmill Closes* is a more "writerly" book than some of my others. It's a little more of a novel, if you will. More of a novel in character and mood and place than anything else I'd done. So I was very pleased with that.

Because of the nature of the book, it sets Scudder in present time—the middle eighties—recounting events that happened in the mid-seventies, and in that respect it's a flashback book. It concerns a case—a couple of cases—that happened several years before *Eight Million Ways to Die* takes place. But that still left me thinking that I was done with the series. I could write other books of his remembering and I would still be no closer to being able to advance the series.

Again, I thought I was done. The only thing that changed that was the passage of time. It certainly wasn't the clamoring of the world, because that makes no sense. That might make me *inclined* to write a book, but if it doesn't work, it doesn't work. Then I was riding a train from Luxor to Cairo, suffering badly with dysentery and insomnia. Insomnia was sort of inevitable on this train, especially given the dysentery. Mine and everyone else's. And I thought of how to do it, and the basic plot notion was one I'd already considered for a Scudder book and had gotten nowhere with before; a couple of chapters and out. This time I had the feeling that I had the sense of the book, and I was able to write it.

And there's no way to account for that. The only supposition I can make is that enough time had passed so that some element of the unconscious mind figured out how to do it. And once I'd written *Out on the Cutting Edge*, my agent offered it at auction, and during the auction he asked, "Would you be comfortable with a two-book contract? Are you going to be able to write more about the character?" And I said, "Yes. I expect to sit down and start another in a couple of months. I already know what the next one is going to be."

Since then I've not really had any trouble writing about Scudder each year. I don't know how long that will be the case. Series often run their course. At least the ones I've written have seemed to. You mentioned earlier that I began the Scudder series after having been writing professionally for, whatever, about sixteen years, I suppose. I think that's been very much to my advantage in the series, that's true.

Writers in the mystery field are under so much pressure now to write books in series that, typically, the first book they ever write is the first book of a series, and the writer finds himself locked into writing the same book over and over, or the same character over and over, before he knows what the hell to do—has mastered the art of writing. I don't think it's very easy to grow doing that, and I think the author gets locked into a character conceived of by an immature writer. I think it's a big mistake.

I've know some writers who feel really handcuffed to a character, and they say, "But my publisher wants more." No writer is going to get anywhere until he learns not to give people what they want, but to make them want what he wants to give them.

EB In Stephen King's introduction to the reprint of the first Scudder book, *Sins of the Fathers*—which is the first hardcover—he makes quite a thing about Scudder being a character with no gimmicks, "No Cats," as he says. What he meant, of course, was that Scudder avoided the trite gimmicks of tradition for some truly original quirks, like his tithing thing. He gives 10 percent of his income to the first church he finds with an open door. Do you have any recollection of where that idea came from?

LB Just seemed like something he might do, that's all.

EB Later, when he reaches a turning point in his own life, he changes from giving it to churches to giving handouts to people on the street.

LB One thing that's been true in this series—and some other people have done this too, but it is certainly not standard in detective fiction—is that the character changes. That was not true of the heroes in classic private-eye fiction. It was certainly not true in the early series mysteries, Ellery Queen, Hercule Poirot, or any of those, where the character was largely a device. Nor was it standard in hard-boiled fiction, by any means.

EB Very little character development.

LB Well, the character is developed maybe, but he doesn't change. He doesn't have a life. He has an episodic life in each book, and he may have trimmings for that and may have peculiar habits and the room he lives in may be furnished with all sorts of quirks and everything else, but there's no sense of change.

Because the Scudder books themselves operate on a pretty basic level of reality, for the character to change—for his life to evolve—was part of the reality for me. Now, when I wrote the first book, I thought he would never change. I thought, this is a series, and this is how we'll do it, and here he is, and this is his life, and thank you very much. But that didn't ring right, and he gradually did change. Of course, the sea change is at the conclusion of *Eight Million Ways to Die.* But even since sobriety, his life has evolved and changed considerably.

So there are things that he may do that he outgrows. Somebody recently at a signing—reading—said that she noticed in the recent books, he doesn't mention the child he killed by accident, and how bad that had been as a propellant in the acceleration of his drinking and the breakup of his marriage and the end of his career and all that. She said he mentioned it in all of the early books and now he doesn't mention it, and I said, "Well, I think he got over it."

EB Time passes in books just as in real life.

LB I think he got over it, yeah. If he hadn't, there would have been something wrong. Of course, he's gotten over it. And he's gotten over other things, too. So, to the extent that I try to figure out what it is I'm doing here, it seems to me that I'm writing the episodic autobiography of someone who doesn't happen to exist in reality, a fictional character. I think of it that way.

EB He certainly comes to life. I do find it hard to imagine somebody so nonjudgmental. I mean, most of us have strong likes and dislikes, a sense of moral outrage, but he allows the people around him a lot of freedom, perhaps because of all that's happened to him. To have a prostitute for a girlfriend and a killer for a best pal takes a special sort of person. There is a wonderful exchange between Bernie and his lady friend in *Burglars Can't Be Choosers* where he says, "There's all kinds of honest." That novel was published the year after the first Scudder, by the way. Bernie might well have had Matt in mind when he said, "He's a different kind of honest."

LB You know, you hear a lot about the private detective in fiction as being "a man with a code," which I've always found a curious phrase. A code that he must sit around and decipher with his Captain Midnight decoder ring, I don't know.

I know there's one fictional private eye who even has conversations with his girlfriend about his code. To my great satisfaction I've never in life met anyone who has conversations about his code, and I hope not to. Anyway, the idea is clear that the private detective has his particular morality all worked out, and that way he knows what he likes and doesn't like and what he'll do and won't do. I don't know a lot of people like that, either.

I don't know a lot of people with a clear code like that—of any sort. Scudder makes it up as he goes along. That's what I do. That's what most of the people I know do, one way or another. There may be some underlying precepts there, but figuring out what to do next is the chief challenge we're given in this life. So I think Scudder makes it up as he goes along and he isn't necessarily bothered by the things we're brought up to be bothered by.

One thing I think is true of every viewpoint character—the ones I write, anyway—is that they are the person I would be if I were them. Though Scudder's attitudes and beliefs and behavior are not identical to mine by any stretch, that's what I'd be if I were Scudder.

EB I understand. Then Scudder's tolerance does reflect, to some extent, a place you've reached in your life?

LB Well, I've known a lot of people who have done stuff of one sort or another and I've found that my affection or lack thereof is not necessarily proportionate—it doesn't mesh with what they have or haven't done. That's not that much different from Scudder.

I remember, years ago—maybe thirty years ago—I read John O'Hara's *From the Terrace*. It came out in 1960, and I think that's when I read it. And I remember the revelation came to me that there weren't really any good guys and bad guys. There were people you were prepared to recognize as bad guys because they were in an adversarial relationship with the hero—at least at one stage, although relationships change. But that didn't mean that they were bad guys. And gradually I have come to believe that there aren't any villains except in context.

I think if I wrote a book that really worked—worked completely—that would be clear. In *A Walk Among the Tombstones* there are some very, very nasty people, and even there, with the ultimate villain in that, there is one exchange where a sort of conversational window of opportunity opens and the humanity of the person is very briefly revealed and then that window is slammed shut again and all you really see after that is all that you really saw before—the psychopathic aspect. So, even there, with the psychopath scenario—a difficult lot to be around—there's a person there. Even with psychopaths, there's a person present and they usually got that way because somebody beat the shit out of them or buggered them a lot when they were three years old. You know, that's usually what happens.

The villain usually, if you trace it back far enough, was a victim himself, one way or another. Scudder is disinclined to judgment, and when he must act, it's either because that's what his role in this proceeding is, or it's certainly done without a great deal of passion, you know. I think the execution at the end of *Slaughterhouse* is just that, an execution. It's dispassionate.

EB He says in a couple of the early books that he would rather not work for somebody he likes. I think he phrases it that it's easier to take money from somebody you don't care for. He's very dispassionate. As he gradually comes back from this dark night of the soul he's been going through, some of the other characters almost seem to be going in the other direction.

Scudder has definitely become more normalized in the recent books. At least his despair seems to have diminished and he seems more comfortable with himself. Now, is he going to have trouble relating to his old cronies? Mick Ballou, his friend at Grogan's, for example, is still pretty much a calculating, cold-blooded killer. And I see the relationship with Elaine developing, and I wonder if, after so many years in the life, she can be unscarred enough, still enough of her own person, to carry on a successful relationship.

LB Well, I don't find that. We'll see. Lewis Lapham was interviewing Robert Parker and me on television, and he asked Parker if Spencer and his girlfriend would ever get married. Parker said, no, he didn't think so. They could go on like the pair on the Grecian urn, but wouldn't catch each other. Then Lewis asked me if Scudder and Elaine ever get married, and I said, "They could and they may, but they won't live happily ever after. Once you get to happily ever after you're done writing."

One of the things that keeps me writing is to find out what will happen next. The 1993 Scudder book, *The Devil Knows You're Dead,* is very much about ongoing developments in Scudder's personal life and very much about relationships.

EB Particularly in the Scudder books you don't seem to have been especially preoccupied with the puzzle. I suppose that has been something of a trend in recent crime fiction, mystery fiction, altogether these days. In the Scudder books in particular the mystery seems to be secondary to the character.

LB You almost have to choose, if you're going to take this whole business seriously. You have to choose between an intricate puzzle and a high level of reality. If the puzzle is really intricate and involved—even if it's realistic and even if you don't have serious poisons from Malaysia and shit—it's very difficult, because as soon as you transform the book into an intellectual exercise, you lose the realism. So that's a problem. Also,

I'm not that good at, or interested in, intricate puzzles. It's just not generally a real-world phenomenon.

EB There is no real-life Nero Wolfe.

LB No, there isn't. Of course not. And most of the time when you have to try and figure out who did it, it's not someone who was on the scene in the beginning. Now, *Tombstones* is not a mystery, but, as in most of the books, what's required is detective work, and that's something a little different. That's knowing that some stranger is out there who has done certain things—committed some crime—and trying to find out who he is, trying to find a name and a face to go with these deeds.

There's no puzzle to solve, but it's still detective work, you know. That often is the way it's been in the various books. In *Boneyard* there's never any mystery. It's really an adventure novel.

EB Matt is such a minimalist, he doesn't have any hobbies or pastimes. One thing he knows a lot about and seems to have some feeling for is boxing. Is that something you share?

LB Yeah, we share that.

EB I know it's of relatively little significance or importance that the geography is right in Hillerman's Navajo books. The geographical reality of novels is a moot point. But obviously your knowledge of and love of Manhattan and the boroughs has a lot to do with the success and the realism of the Scudder books. Do any of the bars and other places actually exist?

LB Sure. Some of them.

EB Is there a Paris Green?

LB No. There are places that exist and places that don't. In the early books, almost every place I named was real, but, as I pointed out at the end of *Boneyard,* most of them are gone. The landscape changes at a really startling rate here. A certain number of the places that are mentioned exist. Some of them exist but I call them something else, and some of them are complete fabrications. Armstrong's, of course, exists, but, as chronicled in the books, moved a block west. I don't get there too often because it's not a neighborhood I'm in that often. I get there a few times a year. Sometimes when Lynne and I go to something at Lincoln Center we'll stop there for a late bite afterwards. And the last time I saw Jimmy, he was talking about how occasionally somebody comes into the place from having read about it, and he said the most remarkable thing was when a group of Japanese tourists came in and said they came there because of my books. The Scudder books are quite popular in Japan. They came for that reason, and they wanted to take pictures of everything. They took pictures of Jimmy, and they took pictures of themselves with Jimmy, and he said it was really quite delightful.

So there's lots that's accurate. The thing is, some people expect the books to be more geographically accurate than they are. From *A Walk Among the Tombstones* I got a letter from a fellow in Albany who had lived in Bay Ridge in Brooklyn twenty years ago, complaining that I had Irish bars and such on Fifth Avenue. There wouldn't be any on Fifth Avenue, but there would be on Fourth and on Sixth—whatever the hell it was. He said, at least that's the way it was when I lived there twenty years ago. First of all, that was twenty years ago, and secondly, who cares? You know I am not writing a guidebook in that respect.

The fact that one avenue in some part of Brooklyn is more residential and less commercial I don't think matters. Or what number I give the avenue, for heaven's sake. And I don't make myself nuts checking to see whether a street in another borough is one way eastbound or westbound, because who cares. It's silly. I do try and get everything as right as I can. Frequently I'm out of town when I write the books. I usually go away to write, and while I will take some maps along, I rely more on my memory. I will often have walked around the neighborhoods where I know I'm going to set something beforehand. But I don't know that much about what's going to happen in my books, and frequently there'll be a scene that I had no plans for, so I do the scene and if I feel the need to, I check it out afterwards. It usually works.

I think that New York is very much a presence in the books. New York is one of the things my books are about. That's not true in all of the books, but in some more than others. That's why I found it really unfortunate that the film they made of *Eight Million Ways to Die* was set in L.A., because it was specifically a New York book in a lot of ways.

The Burglar books are also very New York, but it didn't bother me at all that the movie of *Burglar* was set in San Francisco—you just move the story there and it works fine. It's just a different setting. But the other one I thought was unfortunate.

EB As we have touched on here and there, perhaps more than in the past, the popularity of mystery fiction comes from a very strong sense of reality, and I suppose if you're writing about an area that you know well and like, that comes through in a very palpable way. I think that makes a big difference in a novel.

LB Evan Hunter, with the McBain 87th Precinct books, made the conscious decision right at the beginning to call New York something else and tilt the city sideways and let his geography just happen. That was a very wise decision for him.

EB Wasn't that a convention of thirty years ago?

LB Not really. You could do that as much today.

EB Like the convention of avoiding specific brand names?

LB Not necessarily. He certainly could have called his city New York and it would have been fine. But the thing is, he saved an awful lot of legwork over an awful lot of years by making up the geography. You don't have to check anything. You don't have to worry about how neighborhoods change. You don't have to keep up with it.

There's a fellow who writes books set in Indianapolis, and he himself has been living in England for quite a few years now. His Indianapolis is not the one you'll find if you drive over there and look at it, because he doesn't know what Indianapolis is like anymore. That can happen. So if you're going to call a place by name, you have to stay fairly close to it. One thing that's been very good for me is that I really do stay close to New York.

I was talking to another writer recently—a successful writer—and I was saying, "Well, it's easy enough to get there riding the subway." He said, "I never take the subway." And I thought, You're really missing something. I take subways and buses all the time, and I walk around the streets all the time, and I sit around in coffee shops all the time, and I know that that's important for the kind of books I write.

EB Perhaps more important than the specific geography—the thing an outsider couldn't fake—is the attitude, the personality of a city, its behavioral quirks. People in New York do at least a few things in a way they're only done in New York by New Yorkers. How they stand on queue for example. I think they tend to be far less stupidly polite here because there's no time to give everybody their correct turn, and that's something that you probably deal with unconsciously but it would be hard to fake.

LB Yeah. A writer could encounter that once and know it, I suppose.

EB But you couldn't do it without having learned it sometime. You could probably give me some examples of peculiarities of the New York personality.

LB Maybe not. I wouldn't know them. They wouldn't seem peculiar to me, would they?

EB Back to Scudder. In contrast to his being so nonjudgmental, Scudder is somewhat obsessed—certainly somewhat preoccupied—with random, senseless violence in modern life, and he often comments on the bizarre scenes that he reads about in the paper.

LB Well, one thing I should mention is that his preoccupations vary from book to book, depending on what's on his mind. And because they vary, usually that turns out to be one of the things the book is about. For example, in *Eight Million Ways to Die*, specifically, he's very much aware of violence and he's each day reading the paper and commenting on what he sees there. That hasn't been so much the case in the other books. That was pretty much specific to that book. And I don't know why he was doing that that way. I know that I was living up in Washington Heights when I wrote the book, and I would work during the day and then would, at the end of the day's work, come down to the Village.

And so every day I would pick up a copy of the *Daily News* before I got on the subway, and I would take the A train down to Fourth Street, and on the ride I would read about one outrage after another and those would be the ones specifically that I would mention the next day. The city never failed me. It always supplied something for Scudder to read and remark about.

I had to read the book later to find out what it was about, because I don't always know what I'm doing while I'm doing it. It seems that as I write, the books are about their plot, and they're also about something else that I'm not really aware of at the time.

Eight Million Ways to Die was about its plot—about the solution of a string of murders. It was also about that stage of Scudder's alcoholism. It was about that. It was also about the frailty of human life. That's very much what it's about, and I wasn't aware that that was a theme until the book was finished. I think that's how it should be. I think when a writer sits down and says the theme of this book is—If you already know, why write the thing?

When the Sacred Ginmill Closes was about male friendship, but I didn't know what it was about while I was writing. The various books have different subthemes, and yes, the reign of violence *is* a preoccupation of Scudder's in that particular book, but I don't know how much it is in others. It's something he notices because what he reads more than anything else is local crime news. That's what he will react to when he's reading, but it's more a factor in that one particular book than in others.

EB What catches his eye or his imagination seems to be a particular type of crime. Violence or sudden death, usually inflicted on some innocent bystander, that is pointless; totally unmotivated, completely undeserved, and therefore meaningless. That seems to really drive him crazy, but it's like trying to solve a puzzle with the wrong pieces—there's never going to be a resolution. But it continues to bother him.

LB It bothers me. I think probably something Scudder struggles with is his perception that the world is a horrible place.

EB The single most traumatic thing that ever happened to him was the accidental perpetration of a similar act of violence—when he caused the death of an innocent bystander. Which makes it even more ironic when he attends the Butchers' Mass with his friend Mick Ballou of the bloody apron. Is the Butchers' Mass a real thing?

LB Yes it is. I don't know that anybody else ever calls it that. For a while I attended that mass, the eight o'clock mass at St. Bernard's. I don't think they have that anymore. It's been dropped, and they have the seven o'clock and then nothing else until the twelve-fifteen at St. Bernard's. But the eight o'clock mass was always attended by a handful of guys working in the meat markets there, who would show up in their work clothes, which is to say their butchers' coats.

EB Do the after-hours places you describe still exist?

LB Well, there have always been places where you can get a drink after hours, whether it was a particular bar that would stay open beyond closing for certain people that they knew or whether it was a place that was just for that. In *A Walk Among the Tombstones* or the next book, there's mention of the fact that one of the long-standing and notorious after-hours joints in the Village was on Houston Street—the top floor of a commercial building on Houston Street—and that those premises are now regularly occupied by an AA meeting. That was an after-hours club that was around for years.

The after-hours in *When the Sacred Ginmill Closes* is described as being located in a small building which has an Irish repertory theater on the ground floor. There is an Irish theater in that neighborhood on the ground floor of a building, but they don't have, or didn't have, an after hours above it.

EB Are they really called blind pigs?

LB I've used that phrase once or twice. That's a term for after-hours places you don't hear much. I don't know if you hear it at all anymore.

EB Inevitably, I have to ask a some general questions about the AA meetings, because there was a period in the books where they became very central to Scudder's life. I suppose there are really as many of them as you describe. You can pop into one virtually any time of the day or night, anywhere? I mean, in a place like New York.

LB Well, certainly. In a large city, yes.

EB And you describe them essentially the way they actually happen?

LB There's a big range of AA meetings, depending on the neighborhood and the nature of the group.

EB One of the best moments in Scudder's metamorphosis comes at the end of *Eight Million Ways to Die.* For several books he has been going to AA meetings, and when it comes his turn to talk, he always says, "My name's Matt. I'll pass." And then he finally stands up and says, "My name is Matt and I'm an alcoholic."

It is such a mundane moment, in a sense, but something he's put off so long, that the reader is really emotionally tuned for it—like the resolution of a chord in music. When he says, "And the goddamndest thing happened. I started to cry," I admit I was a little choked up myself. That was a real moment.

LB Well, as I said, when I started writing the series, I didn't expect Scudder to change. I thought he would be the same hard-drinking guy, living the same life forever, and that's what happened—that's what he was—in the first three books.

The fourth book took a long time to write because I was at a period in my life when I was having trouble finishing things. I would get sixty pages into a book and have trouble figuring out any reason for any of the characters to go on or what they would do when they did. Then I wrote two novelettes about Scudder in probably '76 and '77—around there. It worked fairly well—they were published in *Alfred Hitchcock's*—and I thought a lot about writing another book, but it took awhile. I sat down and wrote it in '79.

There was every commercial argument against doing so, because Dell had meanwhile done nothing with the books and interesting another publisher in the series didn't seem likely. Dell hadn't done anything with the Scudder series. They published those books in '75 and '76, and they had not been successful, and although one of the books got an Edgar nomination for best paperback, a minor critical success like that didn't really mean anything.

So there was all the reason in the world not to expect another publisher to be enthusiastic about a book that one publisher had already not done well with. But I felt it was what I wanted to write, and my agent encouraged me to write whatever I felt good about. In *A Stab in the Dark*, the character began changing. His drinking began to seem more pathological, and at the end of the book he actually goes so far as to walk into an AA meeting and take one look around the room and say, "The hell with this shit" and go out and get something to drink.

After I'd written that, it was clear to me that what I wanted to do in the next book was continue the story, and in *Eight Million Ways to Die* I knew almost going in how I was going to end it. That became clear.

Eight Million Ways to Die was very long for a first-person detective novel. It was just about twice as long as the first three books. *A Stab in the Dark* was a little longer than the first three, but this was twice as long again—ran four hundred and forty pages in manuscript, or more than that—and I wondered whether that would work. That's a long time to have one voice drone in your ear. But there was a lot I wanted to have happen in the book, and I decided just to take whatever length I needed.

EB That book is my favorite of the series, and I've heard other people say the same. I think that should prove a point to publishers—and maybe to writers themselves—that there is a public out there for books that push the boundaries of the genre. *Eight Million Ways to Die* stands as a novel by most anybody's standards. It doesn't have to be in any way stigmatized by the label "murder mystery."

I'm glad it did well. It's well thought of, and it was critically well received, and I hope it encourages publishers to be a little more daring. Today a lot of houses still have page limits and formula restrictions. Many of them won't look at a manuscript over so many pages. So what happens to those special books that transcend the genre?

LB First somebody has to write them. I think worthy books have a way of getting published.

EB I hope so. I'd like to talk a little more about Scudder and AA. With an organization called Alcoholics Anonymous it seemed to me that you had a built-in problem in taking him through the whole process of reaching sobriety. All those meetings he attends and the stories that various characters stand up and tell all seem completely real. You had to keep it realistic and still not violate anyone's privacy.

LB It's fiction. I don't know what I can say beyond that.

EB Without violating anybody's privacy, I assume that those were typical meetings, typical responses.

LB I don't know what's typical and what isn't. As you pointed out, they do call it Alcoholics Anonymous, and a part of what's implicit in that is that my characters are not talking about anything outside of the context of fiction. Just as I am disinclined to say whether I am or am not a member of Alcoholics Anonymous, because since there is an AA tradition against identifying oneself as a member, I feel that whether I am or am not, that it is certainly in the spirit of that tradition for me not to say. Similarly, I feel it's in the spirit of that tradition not to say where the stories came from—whether I ever heard them or made them up.

EB   There's a period there for several books where he attended a lot of meetings, popping in and out, sometimes several in a single day. It's very compelling material, and I found the process fascinating. I was also taken by the fact that sometimes Matt is fairly critical. Even after he's part of the program and struggling very hard, there are days when he talks about tuning out the speaker. A couple of times he actually thinks it's bullshit. That's one of the things that makes him so real.

One of the things that I think you have consistently done over the years is have your character play against type. You come up with characters who have very contradictory aspects, like a wise-cracking, rather likable bookseller who moonlights as a burglar and who is completely shameless about his vocation and the thrill it gives him.

In the short story "Answers to Soldier," you have a hit man who has this fantasy of a middle-class existence. Can you tell me anything about where Keller came from?

LB   The thought I had consciously in mind when I wrote the first story about Keller, "Answers to Soldier," was the idea of a hit man who, almost against his own will, gets acquainted with his target and then finds himself with the unpleasant prospect of having to kill somebody he knows.

That's what I had in mind when I started out. I sat down and the story found its own direction. Keller is a sort of wistful character, who actually, probably, is closer in personality type to Bruce J. Friedman's *Lonely Guy* than to anybody else. He's just sort of a lonely guy. That's the way he developed, and the story just worked fine, the way it came out. It was curious, in that it's a pretty complicated little story and I never changed a word. I wrote it in one draft and that's what you see. It just worked very nicely. They don't always work out quite that well.

I never thought I'd write more about Keller, because I thought he really does the whole package right there. And then I found out, as occasionally happens, that I was mistaken and that I had more to say about Keller. So there's a story in *Playboy* called "Keller's Therapy," and there's a third and fourth story written. And there will be a book. I'm sure there won't be more than one book. That will do it. But I think there will be a book.

EB This isn't the first, or even the third or fourth, time you've done something like that. Where you create an offbeat character, put him in some weird situation, and then start playing off variations. The Ehrengraf stories come immediately to mind. The idea of a lawyer who is willing to commit a crime to get his client acquitted would appear to be a one-shot deal. Part of Bach's genius comes from the deliciously subtle variations he can work out of the same theme. You sometimes use characters in the same way. You set up a proposition and then tickle it and tinker with it. As though once you have an idea your subconscious immediately starts wondering what else you could do with the same bit.

LB The idea for the Ehrengraf stories was a natural for a series. There are a limited number of things you can do with it, given the nature of the bit, but the idea of a criminal lawyer who gets his clients cut loose by committing criminal acts himself is one with an actual historical antecedent that I wasn't aware of in the Melville Davisson Post stories about Randolph Mason. However, Post reformed Randolph Mason with the passage of time, and Mason mellowed and became more law abiding. Ehrengraf, I'm sure, will never make that mistake. I don't know that there will ever be any more, but as I said, as soon as I finished the first story, I thought he was a natural character to be in other stories if I could think of them. And I thought of seven or eight.

EB That's interesting, because a good deal of my pleasure in reading each new Ehrengraf story comes from the feeling I had from the beginning that it was not a character, clever and intriguing as he was, who had any place to go. The delight of the stories, it seemed to me, was that you could keep coming up with new wrinkles in a wonderfully O. Henry sort of way.

LB I have a feeling that I may not be able to do that anymore.

EB With Keller the same thing is not true. He is, it seems to me, more in the line of Scudder than in the line of Ehrengraf.

LB I don't know how true that is. It's not that realistic a series. But with Keller, he is what the stories are about. With Ehrengraf, they're plotted stories and that's just the way they evolved. With the Keller stories, what happens is most interesting because it's happening to and through Keller, I think.

What we've got now with Keller is a novel in the form of short stories. That's what it is going to be. There will be about ten stories within an overall continuing story line, and—I would hope—some sort of resolution.

EB It seems like a fairly recent phenomenon to have a protagonist who is essentially a bad person, at least in the criminal or legal sense. But we get involved with them all the same and identify with them. You're not the only writer using characters like that.

LB I don't know how recent it is, the use of criminal characters. I'm writing about a charming burglar, and E. W. Hornung was writing those in the last century, with Raffles, the gentleman cracksman.

EB That's not quite so criminal as a hit man.

LB There were the hard-boiled detectives in the early Black Mask stories, like the John Carroll Daly character Race Williams, who was a piece of work. And Sam Spade is committed to only one ethical principle and that's if somebody kills your partner, you should do something about it. But outside of that, he's no upholder of law and order. The only reason he turns her in is he doesn't want to be made a fool of—he doesn't want to get stuck.

EB   He sleeps with his partner's wife, cheats his clients, but he doesn't ever do anything appalling.

LB   He just isn't called upon to do anything appalling. He would do something appalling if there were a reason. I think there's certainly been a tradition of immoral or amoral characters with a somewhat elastic approach to legal nicety.

EB   One other thing I wanted to ask you about Ehrengraf: Does he wear the Caedmon Society tie just as a memorial to the case where he had the extra tie left over, or is there really something behind the Caedmon Society?

LB   He had to go and buy all those damn ties. He feels really good about that tie. There is, to my knowledge, no Caedmon Society, and even in fiction, I don't know what it means. Caedmon was a poet, I think, either Anglo-Saxon or early whatever.

EB   So there's no secret pun there or anything?

LB   No, for heaven's sake.

EB   And the tie is just because he had the leftover ties?

LB   It's because that's the tie he wears on triumphant occasions.

EB   I'd like to talk a little about working methods. I know you've written four books on writing and it's a subject you're a little sick of, but you probably have tricks of the trade that have nothing to do with writing per se but just your own personality quirks, like Hemingway writing standing up or someone else using only number 2 lead pencils or yet another writer with a lucky forty-year-old manual typewriter.

LB It depends. I've approached the writing routine very differently over the years at various times. When I was first writing, I wrote daily, generally six days a week, and put in a fairly regular work day. And I've had various periods in my life when I've written books at various times of the day. As a general thing now, for some years, I've found that it works best if I make writing the first thing that I do in a day, so that I get up and don't really do anything else until I'm done with the day's work, which usually has me writing during the day and sleeping during the night, which is fairly standard.

On one book I can think of, not too long ago, this was switched around some. That was on *When the Sacred Ginmill Closes.* We were also involved in the seminar business at that time, and though it wasn't our seminar season yet, we were doing our promotion and all and enrolling for the next season and selling books and tapes through the mail and that—doing a variety of things that required my work during the day when the post office and other businesses were open.

I tried to get up early in the morning and write on the book, and that wasn't working, and there were just a lot of distractions during the day. So what I finally wound up doing was starting work each night around midnight and writing until four or five in the morning, when I'd go to sleep. I'd get up around ten or eleven in the morning and do the things that had to be done during the day and then lie down, generally, after dinner for a few hours and get up and go to work at midnight.

We were living on Horatio Street in the Village at that time. That was before our move to Florida. This would have been in early '85. Probably January or February of '85. The book took a little over a month to write, as I recall, and it was the perfect book to write at that time of day. It's a late-night, after-hours-joint, bar-closing-time kind of a book, and writing it alone, sitting in the hours between midnight and dawn when the rest of the city was asleep, worked just fine. It was much easier to capture the tone than if I'd been writing it in broad daylight. That one worked very well, but aside from that I generally work days.

One thing that I have done increasingly in recent years, so that it's just about the only way I work, is that I go away to work. I've had the propensity for years that if I got stuck on a book, I'd cope with that by going off somewhere, taking a hotel room in another city and working there. That had always worked well for me, but it never occurred to me to do all my work that way. And in '87 I discovered writers' colonies, like Ragdale and the Virginia Center for the Arts, which are the two that I've been to. There are about a dozen around the country, I guess.

And that was great. They would supply a place to sleep and a place to work and meals—all for a very nominal, affordable fee. And there were other writers there who you could talk to in everybody's off hours or keep your distance from as you pleased. It was acknowledged by everybody that work came first and that a person would not be any more social than he was inclined to be.

I found that very effective, and ever since I've been going to colonies and also, occasionally, creating a one-person writer's colony of my own. The book that I did most recently, I did in San Francisco at a hotel. The book before that, *The Devil Knows You're Dead*, I stayed in New York. The main reason was not so that I'd have access to the city, but there were things going on and I didn't want to pull up stakes and go somewhere else. But I did want the seclusion.

I was going to take a hotel room, which is tougher to do in New York than anywhere else in the country. I couldn't find a hotel that I was willing to be in that was affordable. In fact, there were a couple of hotels I didn't much want to be in that were still going to cost me a hundred dollars a day and I didn't want to spend that. I almost took an apartment, a sublet, but even that was awfully high. And they wanted my fingerprints and my grandmother's maiden name before I could take it. You couldn't just rent it like a hotel room. It was complicated.

And then a friend in Chelsea who had a house with one vacant floor asked me to come stay there. So I did. Even though I was a matter of blocks from my house and I would go home and I would see Lynne every evening, I would sleep in Chelsea so that I could wake up and go straight to work and so that I could isolate it. For me, a lot of the creative process is accelerated and channeled—focused—by being in some degree of isolation.

EB Do you have a habit of doing drafts in your head—thinking about the book for a long time so when you finally sit down to write it goes pretty fast?

LB I don't know to what extent that's true. Early on I didn't think about a book a long time before I sat down and wrote it. I sat down right away and went to work on it. In recent years I'll write a book in a month or two, and I generally write one book a year, so that gives me a lot of discretionary time. And a lot of times when I'm away from my work, I usually note something about the next book and I let it percolate, and by the time I go to work on it, presumably, it will have developed some in my mind.

This doesn't necessarily mean that I know what the plot is. It doesn't necessarily mean that I know who the characters are. I know a certain amount about it, but all of the real work gets done at the keyboard. There's no way around that.

Sometimes I'll know a lot about the book and sometimes I'll know very little. I think it's more a matter of the free time allowing me to internally prepare to do the book than for me to know consciously a great deal about it.

EB I gather from the things I've heard you say and what you've written that you never have been one of those people who like to do an outline or take extensive notes.

LB I have outlined in the past, but I don't do that now. And while I may develop a lot of the plot, I've tended to avoid putting anything on paper because I don't want to concretize anything. I don't want to limit the creative process. I don't want to send myself any subliminal instructions to stop figuring the book out. I'd rather it be fluid as long as possible.

EB Have you ever had that experience that some writers claim where characters just seem to take on a life of their own and do and say unexpected stuff and the author becomes a sort of observer, writing it down as fast as the character tells it?

LB Well, that's a bit of an exaggeration. It's more a matter of intuitive and almost instantaneous knowing of what the character is ready to do or say next, I think. That's what happens. Even if I know a character, it doesn't necessarily mean I always know how he's going to behave or that I know what line he's going to speak next, but it does mean that if I write something on the page and it's right, I know it right away. I know I got it right.

EB That's what Scudder would say—how Bernie would talk?

LB Yeah. Or I know one way or another I don't like it.

EB But you never have that feeling that characters have a will of their own? You don't have direct control?

LB Well, I go one on one, and I try not to lose sight of the fact that the characters that we're talking about are not really more than figments of my own imagination.

I don't know if there's very much more to say. I don't have a routine. I work differently at different times. Just as the books are different, the way they're written is different. I know there's a fascination with writing methods, and I think it's misplaced. I understand it. It stems from the fact that people don't know how writers do it and think if they look at the external circumstances they'll understand the process—and they won't. Any more than what the writer wears is relevant.

It may be interesting, for example, that Cheever got up in the morning, put on a suit and a tie and a hat and rode the elevator down to the basement, where he had an office, where and when he took off the tie and the coat—the tie and the hat anyway—and sat down and wrote. It doesn't have very much to do with what got on the page or how he got it on the page.

I understand the interest, but how I or any writer works has to do with the writer's internal landscape, internal wardrobe, or a whole lot of things that are not visible and cannot be visible and ought not to be visible. I don't think you know a single fresh thing about Hemingway's work by knowing that the son of a bitch stood up while he wrote it. I don't think you know a lot more about Hemingway by knowing that.

How I do it is off the point, but it does vary and it does depend on the circumstances. For years I used a typewriter, and for the more recent books I used a computer. I don't know that there's very much difference. The salient difference to me—one of the main reasons I wanted to use a computer—was that I could carry it on and off of a plane, so that when I want to go someplace to write, I can take it with me easily because the thing only weighs seven pounds. There are other nice things about it, but actually I'm more fond of it for mailing lists and nonwriting functions than I am for the writing, though I like it for that.

Sometimes I hand write. I take a notebook to a café and sit at a table and write by hand. I like to do that, particularly with articles because they are more trouble for me structurally. I like the flexibility it gives me to hand write a draft.

But the time of day I write, the amount of work I try to get done during the day, all of that will vary enormously with the particular book. One of the things that perhaps makes getting away to work effective for me is that I'm completely out of my world and into a world where there's only me and the writing. It isn't so much that there aren't disruptions; it's that there are really no intrusions on thought. The mail doesn't come, I don't run into people I know, the phone doesn't ring, and I'm with myself and the book and nothing else, twenty-four hours a day.

And whatever place I go, I'll live a life that fits that situation. I'll have particular habits that grow up around that. I know Simenon was compulsive that way. He went to a different city and a different hotel for each book. His books were quite short, and it's not inconceivable that he wrote them in the two weeks that he allotted for their completion, because they were terribly short and they did not require a tremendous amount of detailed plotting. He made a fetish of repeating all of his ritual habits. Whatever he happened to do on the first day, he would do identically on succeeding days. He would buy his tobacco at the same kiosk, he would sit at the same café, as if this were necessary.

He also may have been feeding an interviewer a lot of shit, because it doesn't seem to me to have made too much sense. But I do understand living a book and it having its particular universe. This may not have anything to do with the subject or the content of the book, but it's simply the mental space one occupies while writing it.

Ideally, you know, what would be really marvelous is if you could really get inspired and write the entire book in five minutes so that it came out entirely from the same state of mind. The more one can foster that, the better it is. That's one reason I like to write a book in a short overall elapsed span of time, rather than over a course of a year or two years or ten years. That way I am in the same place with it throughout. On the other hand, I must admit that I don't know how necessary this is, because when the book's universe is sufficiently self-contained, none of the rest matters.

For example, the third book I wrote about Evan Tanner was called *Tanner's Twelve Swingers*—unfortunately, but that was the publisher's title for it. I wrote the first fourth of it, something like that, during a time when my first marriage was going into upheaval. It didn't end until some time after that, but it looked as if it were going to. So, when I'd written about a fourth of the Tanner book, I separated from my wife and went to New York for a while, went through a lot of personal trauma, and wound up getting on a plane and going to Ireland, where I stayed two months. The first month I was in a bed and breakfast in Dublin. I rented a typewriter there. I bought a ream of typing paper, which is too long and too thin, in the manner of the nation.

Because part of the book was set in Latvia, I went out and picked up a book at Eaton's on O'Connell Street called *Teach Yourself Latvian*, so the

Latvian in there is authentic. And I wrote the rest of the book in circumstances utterly different from the ones I had occupied before and a self that had been transformed by a very difficult month or two intervening. The book was very full of high drama and low comedy. I finished the book and sent it off.

And as you read it now, I would defy anyone, including myself, to say where the break is. It was manifestly written very much by the same person, although I was certainly in very different circumstances when I wrote the two parts. So I don't know how essential all that is—the perfect working environment—though I have increasingly gravitated toward that.

EB Because you *can* afford to do it in that more comfortable way now?

LB I don't know about that. We're not talking high expenses to go someplace and live in a residential hotel room. We're certainly not talking high expenses to go to a writer's colony. It costs fifteen, twenty dollars a day, and that includes a room and three meals. I can't live that cheap when I'm staying at home.

EB What are the requirements to go to a writers' colony? I would suppose they don't allow unpublished or would-be writers.

LB No, you have to establish legitimacy, and almost all of them get far more applications than they have spaces for, so there's a selection process.

EB One of the first articles you wrote for *Writer's Digest* discussed the gestation and birth of Evan Tanner.

LB Well, the Tanner series evolved gradually. The germ of the concept came to me in '63 or '64. I was still in the Buffalo area when I came across two bits of information that attracted my attention. One was an article I'd read in *Time* magazine about sleep and insomnia, and it mentioned that there seemed to have been several documented cases of people living on no sleep at all. I thought about that and wondered what it would be like to live on no sleep at all and what I would do with the extra hours in the day. Judging from my own use of discretionary time in the years since then, I've decided that if I had twenty-four hours in a day that I was conscious, I would probably waste them just as effectively as I do when I have sixteen or eighteen.

In actual fact, I don't think it would make that kind of difference, but I found it interesting to think about all the things you could do with the extra time. I thought, wouldn't it be interesting to have a character who doesn't sleep?

With that idea in the back of my mind, I was looking up something else in the encyclopedia and discovered that there was still a Stuart pretender to the English throne. The last reigning monarch of the House of Stuart was Anne, who died in 1714, I believe. And then there was James III, as he called himself, the Old Pretender, and finally, Bonnie Prince Charlie, the Young Pretender.

After the Scots were defeated at the Battle of Culloden in 1746, the House of Stuart ceased to be any factor in British politics, although there were still people who drank toasts to "the king over the water" for a while. However, there was still a Stuart pretender, and he was some little German princeling or something of the sort, and I thought this was fascinating. I began to put the two together in my mind and have the idea that this guy who couldn't sleep had, among other things, a passion for the restoration of the House of Stuart to the English throne. It was an idea, but it wasn't an idea for a book, yet. I couldn't think what would happen, and I forgot about it.

Then, when I was in Racine, working at Western Printing in the coin supply division, there was a fellow who had worked there for a while who was back in town, and I got to talking with him and invited him over for dinner. He and I sat up drinking far into the night, and he regaled me with talk about the two or three years that he had spent in Turkey, where he earned a very precarious living, engaging in the illegal activity of smuggling old coins and antiquities out of the country. He had had some really close shaves. This was before the Turkish jails had been immortalized in *Midnight Express,* but even so, one sensed that they were not the sort of place you wanted to hurry off to. And he almost got pulled off a plane one time when he was smuggling a consignment of Roman glass out of the country to Zurich or Geneva.

There was a batch of neat things that he talked about, and he told a story about a couple of guys—I think one of them worked for Aramco—who were trying to find and rescue the gold coins, the gold treasures of Smyrna, which had been supposedly sequestered by the Armenian community after the genocide in 1915. The gold coins were supposed to have been hidden under the stoop or porch of a house in Balahissar, and the two guys finally did find the house and did break in and did discover evidence that the gold had been there, but it was gone by the time they got there.

Well, I listened to all of this, and I woke up the next morning and miraculously remembered the conversation and thought that I suddenly had something for my character to look for—to do—this guy who couldn't sleep and wanted to restore the House of Stuart. And once I had something for him to do, I suddenly discovered that I knew a lot more about the character than I had before, and I wrote the book that became *The Thief Who Couldn't Sleep,* which was the first book about Tanner. I wound up writing seven books about the character and had a lot of fun with it until it just seemed to me that the books were getting labored, and I stopped.

EB Was there any particular influence on that character as a result of the immense popularity of the James Bond character or Matt Helm?

LB I don't think so at all, because in the first book I certainly didn't think of Tanner as a spy or agent or anything. He is simply a guy who has been making his living writing other people's theses and papers for them, and living on the Upper West Side, and learning lots of languages, and belonging to all sorts of mutually exclusive irredentist movements and lost causes. And in the course of the book, he winds up being pursued by the police of a couple of continents and poses as an agent as a way of explaining himself. Then he gets involved in other things, later on.

I certainly didn't think of the book as the first of a series, by any means, and I didn't think of it as in the realm of spy fiction at all. I just thought of it as an adventure book—an urban adventure transplanted. Since I had various acquaintances in New York who were involved in various political splinter groups, the mindset was not difficult to catch.

EB   Tanner becomes very international over the course of the series.

LB   Oh, sure. And he almost always goes to places that I hadn't been, though the settings I had the most trouble with for Tanner were the ones I was most familiar with.

EB   Because you felt like you could just let it be.

LB   Well, sure. The Tanner books are not terribly realistic. I think of them as romps, really. They're tough-minded in spots, but they don't correspond too closely with any world that we know. And I was very, very cavalier as far as research. I rarely went any deeper than the *Encyclopedia Britannica*.

EB   What difference did it make?

LB   That was what I felt. So I suspect the books must read funny to somebody who is familiar with the particular locale. Of course, now everything's changed so much. The first Tanner book was published in '66 or '67, and there has been quite a little change in the globe since then. Look at Eastern Europe.

I get letters every once in a while from people who say, "It's clear that the reason we haven't heard anything about Tanner lately is that he's so busy." What happened, incredibly, is that all of these lost causes and splinter groups and bits of factionalism that were ridiculous when the books were written have been successful all over the place. Who really expected, for God's sake, that groups like the IRA or Croatian Separatists or Slovaks or any of the rest of them would turn out to be viable political forces? Suddenly, all these groups that seemed to have no existence outside the bounds of the Tanner series are killing people and starting wars, and even winning some of them, and it's gotten quite scary.

EB Do you feel you were sort of prescient?

LB No, not really, because it's not what I expected. It was the last thing I expected.

EB How did you come up with all of these lost causes? Some of them were pretty obscure.

LB Yeah. Some of them are obscure. Some of them don't exist at all. But some of them that may seem the most obscure do actually exist.

EB How did you find them?

LB Oh, one finds them. One finds them. It's not that hard. You come across some odd group in a bit of writing somewhere and you just postulate the continued existence of it. You hear about things. I did hear of somebody who avoided military service in the late fifties by accepting a commission in the Lithuanian army in exile, for example. Now, from that to the Latvian army in exile doesn't seem like much of a stretch.

And as I said, certain organizations, like IMRO—the Internal Macedonian Revolutionary Order—very much existed and still do, astonishingly. Every once in a while, they turn up in the paper. I though they were out of business. They had a lot to do with starting the First World War, by the way.

EB Did you know a lot about the Baltic nations for any particular reason?

LB No. Neither the Baltics nor the Balkans. I did wind up having a Latvian girlfriend in the early seventies, but that was after I wrote the book. Which is typical for me. I seem to do most of my research after I've written a book.

EB You spoke earlier about how a failed plot for the Scudder series became the first Bernie Rhodenbarr book, but we didn't talk about where the character himself came from. I love his sense of humor. You also have a little fun with antiquarian book dealers. Why did you give Bernie a day job as a bookseller?

LB It didn't start that way. In the first two books he doesn't have a day job. It's an interesting thing with a series, it frequently takes a few books to find out what you've got.

Although Rex Stout had a pretty good sense of Nero Wolfe, the house, and everything else right from *Fer de Lance*, Wolfe's character took a few books to settle out. He's something of a windbag in the early books. It frequently takes a while for a writer to find out what he's got. *Burglars Can't Be Choosers* was not conceived as the first book of a series, and at the end of the book there's no reason for there to be more books about the character. The only reason there *were* more books about the character is I really liked the voice and I really liked the character and I just sat down and wrote a second one.

Having written two books about Bernie, I began to have more of a sense of the character. It was time to furnish the rooms a little. He doesn't especially have a life in the first two books. By the third book, he has a life. I thought running a secondhand bookstore would be an interesting occupation for him, and that's where he got the bookstore and that's where he got the best friend.

That's where Carolyn Keiser comes in. I thought it would work wonderfully to make her a lesbian, because that way it's a buddy relationship but it's also energetically a male-female relationship, and I liked that a lot.

EB I think that works well.

LB Yeah. There were some people that thought it was a bad idea. I think my agent thought that it was a bad idea, that it would put people off and stuff.

EB Well, it's politically sensitive, I suppose, but I think she's a rather likable character, so I don't see anybody getting too excited.

The first book in the Scudder series has an interesting dedication, and, though I know such things aren't directed to the reader, it's provocative, suggesting there's a story behind it. The dedication of *The Sins of the Fathers* reads: For Zane, who was present at the creation, and in memory of Lenny Schecter, who introduced me to Scudder.

LB Right, it's not directed to the reader. Lenny Schecter wrote a book called *On the Pad*. Lenny Schecter was a reporter for the *New York Post* and also, interestingly, the official scorer at Mets games. And he wrote a book with a policeman that gave me an insight into a certain aspect of a certain kind of police mentality, which had something to do with the formation of the Scudder character. It doesn't fit that well. There's no person that Scudder's based on.

EB Tell me something about the great buffalo hunt, your search for places called Buffalo or with Buffalo in the name. How did you happen to come up with the idea of seeking out places called Buffalo?

LB It was fun, but I feel like I've talked about it so much. I grew up in Buffalo, New York, of course, and growing up there I knew that there were several other towns named Buffalo, and while I was writing *Random Walk*, which involved spending a lot of time with a detailed atlas, I discovered that there were really more places named Buffalo than I thought, and by the time I was done writing the book, I had found about twenty places named Buffalo. Around this time Lynne and I began thinking about leaving Florida and taking a rambling drive around the country, and we weren't sure what we would do while we were doing that. And I said, very tentatively, you know, maybe we could go to some of these other Buffalos, since there were twenty of them.

I said, "I think we should go to some of them." Lynne drew herself up very straight and said, "I think we should go to all of them." So I decided to plan accordingly, and I started doing some more research with atlases, and by the time we were ready to leave in February of '88, I knew of forty. At this stage of the hunt, five years later, of those forty, we've been to sixty-five and know of about twenty or twenty-five more.

As you can see, it's sort of like subatomic particles; looking for them causes others to spring into existence. It gave our travels a wonderful illusion of purpose. Obviously it didn't make any difference in the overall scheme of things whether we got to these burgs or not. But it gave us a way to decide whether to turn left or right whenever we came to that sort of fork in the road, and gave us a marvelous sense of accomplishment. And it was fun. It got us around the country.

We still have not by any means concluded this hunt, although we're willing for it to take its time. In late June we're planning to drive into northern New England, and there is a Buffalo in Maine. Very few people know about it because it's not on most maps, but I know where it is and we'll probably get there.

EB By the time you get to sixty-plus, are some of these places really not towns?

LB Many of them don't exist. Many of them are ghost Buffalos. There was a town there once. Some of them are just cemeteries. Buffalo Gap in Saskatchewan is a cemetery. It has a nice sign and everything, but that's all that's left. Buffalo Springs, North Dakota, in the southwest corner of the state, doesn't exist—there's still a sign at the railroad siding, but nothing else. There's no other evidence of the town. You have to leave the road and go up to the railroad siding and then you can find the sign. That was a tough one to get.

EB Did you document all this with a camera?

LB Yes, yes. We had a Polaroid camera with us, and we took photos of each other, wearing our Buffalo t-shirts, at every Buffalo we came to. And a bunch of the photos ran in the article that I did for *American Heritage.* The editor there was very clever. He reproduced them as Polaroids with the borders and all, so that they looked like icons, artifacts.

EB So the Buffalo hunt wasn't a single trip but an ongoing journey?

LB No, the Buffalo hunt is a way of life. We're talking long-term commitment. And I love the fact that we seem destined never to run out of them, because we get no closer to our goal. We picked up several in Nebraska last year—certain ghost Buffalos in Nebraska—and found out about any number of others. The number of places in the West that, one time or another, had post offices named Buffalo is probably infinite. And even without getting that esoteric, we've got lots of room here.

EB Did you know when you went through Gallup that you passed a Buffalo?

LB No.

EB Iyanbito. About fifteen miles east of town, it's the next to the last exit before you get to Gallup. Iyanbito is Navajo for Buffalo Springs.

LB No kidding? Lynne would have gone nuts.

EB You started traveling rather young. People travel for all sorts of different reasons. You've traveled at crisis points in your life.

LB Actually, I was thinking that there's an unpublished piece on just that subject, so why don't we include it in the book?

EB I think that's a great idea.

EB I think we've talked about all the series characters except Chip Harrison, so maybe we should pick him up. In the third and fourth books in the series, you got to spoof the detective genre a bit. I think they're quite funny.

LB The first two books, *No Score* and *Chip Harrison Scores Again*, aren't detective stories. The way Chip Harrison came about, I got the idea of doing an erotic young-boy-coming-toward-manhood novel. I think the working title I had on the thing was *Lecher in the Rye*, which makes it clear what we were dealing with, there. Again, it was a nice voice and I had a lot of fun with that first book. I enjoyed the premise that Chip Harrison was the author—that the character had written the book—and it wasn't until the fourth novel in the series that anybody involved in publishing them knew who the author was.

That remained a secret. As a matter of fact, the contracts and copyrights were all in the name of Chip Harrison. I doubt the publishers thought it was true, but a lot of the readers did. I got a lot of mail from adolescents in response to the first book. And it was fun, and I had a good time with it. And again, I wrote the second book because I liked the first. It had done well, too, which made Fawcett receptive when I approached them with the second book. But I just enjoyed doing it.

After two books I realized that I had a problem here—because I would like to do more, but he starts the thing as a seventeen-year-old virgin, and by the end of the second book he's an indeterminate amount older, probably eighteen or nineteen. You can't have him grow up or he loses his character. Some people only like kittens, you know. He was in great danger of growing up, and then there's nothing to do. And there's also sort of nowhere to go, because how many times can you lose your virginity? So I thought, well, I can put him to work for a private detective and then he can stay the same age forever.

EB And he stays sort of permanently sexually frustrated, too. That's always an undercurrent.

LB That's all that interests him. You get much older and that changes, unfortunately. But it was fun. Making Leo Haig a poor man's Nero Wolfe and a great mystery fan himself was a great way to save the series, but it also really made it kind of a one-trick pony. I did two more books, and that was just enough, you know. I couldn't do anymore.

EB It's a very appealing character. He's a send-up of the classic picaresque hero, right out of the mainstream of American literature. A Huckleberry Finn character with a hard-on and an attitude. You make him young, innocent, an orphan on the lookout for the main chance, and bright and clever in spite of his lack of worldly sophistication. I remember reading somewhere in your writing that you don't care for the *faux naif,* and yet that's essentially what Chip is. As is Huck Finn.

He's bright enough to see—and to expose—the stupidity around him, and that's one of the things I like. And unlike most kids that age, he keeps his mouth shut. There are quite a few times in the books, I recall, he would say, "I could see what was wrong with that, but I wasn't going to say anything."

LB This was back in the late sixties or early seventies. Maybe a seventeen year old then was more likely to keep his mouth shut. I don't know.

EB I always put my foot in it. But what about making him an orphan and all that stuff? Your working title already gave a nod to the classic coming-of-age novel *Catcher in the Rye.* That's so especially American, I think. The young boy on his own. There's a definite Horatio Alger element there, and I think he even mentions the Alger hero somewhere in the first book. And his favorite phrase is "a job with a future." The Horatio Alger hero, by pluck and luck, honesty, integrity, and hard work, rises above the circumstances.

LB Well, absolutely. In the first book, the two things he was looking for were to get laid and a job with a future. But that character has appeared throughout literature.

EB Not in quite the same way. I think early American literature was full of this sense of unlimited opportunity, rising above one's station in life. That character in American literature has more optimism, more sense of the future than, say, Joseph Andrews.

LB Well, when you were locked into the "great chain of being" philosophy and the idea that one never rose above one's station, you couldn't very well have someone aspiring to do so. So it's both fairly contemporary and American in that respect, but the idea of a character off to discover the world and himself has been around for a while.

EB Sooner or later I have to raise the ghastly question of pen names. I have read the piece published in *Telling Lies for Fun and Profit* about the pen-name issue, and I'm clear on your position and agree with your arguments in principle. At the same time, Lynn Munroe and several other paperback bibliographers are obviously never going to let this issue rest. Now that you've seen that Lynn Monroe catalogue, have you revised or changed your attitude toward keeping a lid on the pen names?

LB If you mean, what's my response to the catalogue, it's hard to take much umbrage over the fact that people like one's work enough to care. On the other hand, as I said in the piece I did for Jim Seel's bibliography, I'm just not inclined to either fan these flames or acknowledge, confirm, or deny in any way.

I don't regard those books as mine, really. At the time I didn't put my name on them for a reason, and I don't really want to do so now. For innumerable reasons, they don't always even feel like my work. Some of them were very heavily edited and spliced around and things like that. Most of the names that I used at one time or another were also used by other people at one time or another. In some instances I would be hard put to tell you who's who.

Their reasoned analysis in the catalog is sometimes right and sometimes not. Their statements from other writers about who ghosted what and who didn't are sometimes right but sometimes not. There are areas I saw there that I wouldn't dream of straightening out, but they're wrong. Not everybody's memory is always accurate. The day may come when I write a tell-all autobiography and clear this up as well, but if so, I'll save it for then. Memoirs are an interesting thing. They should be written when you're still young enough to remember but old enough not to give a fuck. I'm still the first, but not quite the second.

EB Honestly, I have no interest whatsoever in getting into what you did or didn't write—exposing any pen name or particular title. But they're of special interest. Obviously, this was very early in your career, and you were involved in the project with people who were then your friends and have remained your friends all these years.

LB Some, yes.

EB And, in fact, there were several writers involved, apparently, with recognizable names, including some from science fiction, as well as Donald Westlake, who has had some things to say on the subject. At the time it must have been kind of a fun thing and an exciting thing to be involved in, and there appear to have been a lot of in-jokes and mutual clowning around. There were a couple of things Munroe and his colleagues turned up that I would like to ask about in sort of general terms.

For one, what was the joke about "The Sound of Distant Drums?" Even assuming that wasn't your joke alone, it seems to be a running gag through the books.

LB The only significant thing about anything like that is that it kept recurring. There was nothing to it. That's one reason why I suppose there are probably an awful lot of dead writers who find it similarly frustrating somewhere in the afterworld when the Modern Language Association is explaining what they did or didn't mean when they said "good morning." It's about on a par with that. One of the maddening things about this whole business is that people find significance where there is none. There was no significance. Someone used that as the name of a play one time. Some people went on using it. It wasn't to any purpose. There was nothing particularly funny about it.

EB I think it was Robert Frost who said that critics were welcome to find any significance they wanted to in his poetry. Anything they liked.

I think a lot of people would like to know if the famous poker game ever happened or is that just one of those legends? The night a group of you wrote a book, one chapter at a time.

LB Well, I've written about the poker game. It happened. It's become a story that I hear wrong so often that I really ought to tell it myself. At a party I heard an agent I know telling all about it and how he was there and he took a turn and he did this and that—he wasn't there.

I was there. I know. He wasn't there. I don't know whether he believes it or whether he just figures it makes a better story in the first person, but he's full of shit. I've heard a lot of things about the poker game, and I suppose it *is* legendary by now. I don't know if it needs to be. There were a batch of us who played poker and some of the people in the game were also writing sex novels at the time, and other people who didn't play cards were writing the same books.

We thought we'd get together a game one night composed just of people who were writing the sex books. If we had half a dozen of them, and if each writer did two chapters in the course of the evening, when we were done we'd have a book, and we would have written an entire book in one night without anybody having to give any real time to it. That would work. I forget whether there were five or six. I think there were six, and five played and one wrote. I think that was the arrangement.

We did this for a while, until one of the people in the group said that he wanted to do his two chapters in a row. He was concerned about his ability to stay up that late. And he wasn't really a card player anyway. He played a few hands until it was his turn to go up, I guess. He went up, and he was there for awhile, and he did both of his chapters. It must have been like forty pages of text. Then he said good-bye to everybody and went away.

Well, one of the reasons he was able to stay up that late, we found out later, was that he'd swallowed some speed before he went upstairs. So he did, indeed, write forty pages, picking up on whatever the story line was at that point and going from there. We were doing this, of course, without an outline. The problem—the plain fact—was that he'd written forty pages that didn't make any sense. He had sentences and there were paragraphs, and there was dialogue and all of that. It parsed, but it didn't make any sense.

Then the guy who followed him was the newest of the group to these books and had the least self-confidence. So instead of looking at this and saying, "Wait a minute, this shit doesn't make any sense," he was up there for three hours trying to write a chapter that would logically follow from it. So that by the time dawn broke, the book wasn't finished and it wasn't anything. So we let that go and then when one of our number sickened and died a year or two later—very young—we somehow or other cobbled together an ending for the book, and it sold with the proceeds going to his widow. I don't know if it ever actually appeared. I certainly have never seen it. I wouldn't recognize it anyway. I have no idea what it may have been about, at any stage in its development.

Very early on in my career I got a questionnaire from *Contemporary Authors,* and I filled it out. This must have been in '62 or somewhere around there. I had one or two books out, you know, and I decided I'd fill it all out. On the form it asked for avocational interests, and I thought, what will I put? Up to that point I filled the questionnaire out completely straight—and I put, "Has an extensive collection of old subway cars." It also asked if you would like to hear from other people that had the same interest—correspond—so I said, "I would be very interested in corresponding with other subway car collectors, especially anyone possessing any of the old wooden cars from the Myrtle Avenue elevated line." You know what the size of a subway car is? How could anybody collect even one of them?

EB Where would you put them?

LB Right, right. You'd be in several Western states. So I just sent this off and I forgot about it—I quite completely forgot about it. Two years later, early '64, I was buying a car, and we made the deal, discussed the trade and everything, and the salesman was going to run the paperwork. The following day, when I come in to pick up the car, the salesman looks at me across the desk and says, "Where do you keep your collection of subway cars?"

Now, mind you, this is two years after I filled out this questionnaire, and I had never before that heard of *Contemporary Authors*. I never looked for it in libraries. I knew nothing about it except that I'd filled out this questionnaire two years before. I looked at him and I said, "What the hell are you talking about?" It turned out that when he found out I was a writer, he wanted to check my bona fides, so he went to the library and he looked me up and he read that entry.

Because one reference book follows another, I'll occasionally come across that little item in some other source. I never did get any correspondence from people with any of the old wooden cars from the Myrtle Avenue el.

EB Which is the book in your bibliography that doesn't exist?

LB When I was working at Western Printing, it was planned that I would prepare a guidebook of Australian coins, and on some questionnaire or other I must have listed it as pending, and periodically I'll see that listed among my nonfiction books. I didn't write it, and I don't know if anybody else ever wrote it.

EB Do you have any sort of closing words on your career at this point? I know you hate it when fans ask about your future plans for series characters, whether or not you'll ever write another Evan Tanner, but I'm happy that you revived Bernie Rhodenbarr for another adventure.

LB I'm pleased with that too. It's very rare that I know what I'm going to do next. Either in private life or in writing, quite frankly, but before I went up to San Francisco and wrote *The Burglar Who Traded Ted Williams*

I was in the extremely unusual position, for me, of knowing what my next three books were going to be. Since one's written, I know, essentially, what the next two are going to be. But I don't expect always to know that far in advance. I can't remember that ever happening before. But I know that I feel comfortable with the idea of writing at least one more book about Bernie, and I know that I want to go on writing about Scudder for as long as I can. In terms of my own endurance with a series, it's hard to know how long that is. A series can't always go on forever.

It's also important for me to have some variety—for Scudder not to be the only thing that I write—or I'm afraid I'll go stale on it faster.

I would like to do more short stories than I do. It probably seems like I have a large body of work in short stories, but when you factor in the number of years I've been doing them, it isn't that many, though there have been quite a few in recent years. A problem for me—well, I don't know if it's a problem, but a fact of life—is that for some time now the only reason to write a short story is that I want to. There's no compelling economic reason to write a short story.

Everything I write, *Playboy* gets first look at, and their payment for a short story is generous and worth the effort, but they don't take that many and you can't write a story with the expectation that it's going to go to a market like that. And beyond that, there's just no depth to the short-story market. You're writing for pocket change. There's not an economic incentive. This may be good for me in that I only write a short story if I really like the idea and if I really want to write it. In fact, I have portions of short stories around the house that I wrote a few pages of—sometimes more than a few pages—and decided that they didn't really quite work, so I just dropped them.

In the years when I was starting out as a writer, I would have found a way to finish them. They might even have been published, but they'd have been inferior. I'd rather not do any more inferior work than I have to.

EB Obviously short stories have been an important part of your writing from the beginning. I think it's interesting, in that you have managed to keep some series characters alive by writing short stories about them between books, or even after a long layoff, like the Scudder stories. Even after a long gap.

LB That's true. There were also two Scudder novelettes along the way that probably kept him alive *for me.* I don't think it affects the readers, particularly, but it's a way of keeping the stuff alive for me. I think that's been true. The Bernie Rhodenbarr story in *Playboy* is an example. I don't know that it kept the series alive, but it reassured me that the character was still alive.

EB You're fortunate in that what little market there is for short stories is accessible to you because you're an established name. The odds are better that you're going to publish your story now than if you were just starting out.

LB You would think so. The last time I wrote a batch of short stories was in the summer of '89. I was in Virginia, and I had gone there with the intention of writing a book, though it didn't work out that way. This was at the Virginia Center for the Arts, the colony there. I wrote a chunk of a book, which ultimately turned out to be *A Dance at the Slaughterhouse,* and I realized that I had the wrong start on it.

While the hundred and eighty pages that I wrote were a good thing for me to have done, I wasn't going to be able to use anything that I had written. Though by having done that, I got a handle on what the story was going to be.

Anyway, there I was with three or four more weeks booked at the colony and nothing to write. So I decided to write some short stories. I wrote a batch of short stories. They went very well. And two of the stories that I wrote there went to *Playboy.* I wrote the first Keller story, "Answers to Soldier," there, and I wrote "The Burglar Who Dropped in on Elvis" there. And I wrote about four or five other stories, including several that I thought really worked well.

One was "Someday I'll Plant More Walnut Trees," which was a woman's viewpoint story, which, when it appeared in *Some Days You Get the Bear,* was singled out in several of the reviews. The critics really liked it. That one didn't sell anywhere. I could not sell it anywhere. It was too tough for the women's magazines.

EB   It reminded me of some of Daphne Du Maurier's stories.

LB   It was too strong for the women's magazines. It was female viewpoint, so of course it wasn't a *Playboy* story. So I sent it to *Ellery Queen,* which I really thought of as the market of last resort because I wanted it to go someplace that would pay decently for it and give it a lot of exposure because I really loved the story. Anyway, the market of last resort was *Ellery Queen's Mystery Magazine* and Eleanor Sullivan, who must have bought virtually everything I sent her for several years, including at least one story I thought was inferior and I was surprised that she took.

She didn't take "Someday I'll Plant More Walnut Trees." She rejected three stories in a row—for a nickel-a-word market. She rejected that and she rejected "The Tulsa Experience," which I thought was an awfully solid story, and she rejected one or two others. I wondered if she'd stopped liking *me* or what it was. It was strange. But for one reason or another they didn't work for her at the time she read them.

So there's no certainty. It's easier for me, I'm sure, to get short stories published, and I do get inquiries from *Original Anthologies,* and if I have stories lying around I send them. And that's nice, you know—it was a long time coming.

I wanted to sell to *Ellery Queen's Mystery Magazine* from the time I started writing stories back in '57, '58. But I didn't sell a story to them until 1976.

EB   When a story collection like *Some Days You Get the Bear* comes out, aren't the sales somewhere close to a novel at this point, and doesn't that sort of make up for the trouble?

LB   It doesn't sell as well as a novel by any means, though it's doing better than expected. There's a belief in the business that readers don't much like short stories and a lot of them do resist them. But they will follow a writer if they like his work enough. It's hard to know sometimes whether the readers like the writer or they just like one character of the writer's. And my Scudder books have had increasing sales with each book, so it's clear to my publishers and to the book trade that there is a following for Scudder.

Whether the following is just for me when I write Scudder or for me generally, they don't know. It's turning out that the short-story collection is selling a lot better than anybody thought, which would suggest that there is a following independent of the character there. And that people who normally just buy novels are buying the story collection.

EB   Short stories can really be wonderful, but if I have any objection to most mystery novels, it's that the books in the genre traditionally have been very short. I like novels to develop, to explore the terrain, to take some time. I don't buy very many short-story anthologies, but I do go out and buy yours.

LB   It will probably end up with a third to half the sales of a novel. I have a feeling a lot of people will decide to not buy it because they can wait for the paperback, and they wouldn't wait for the paperback of the new Scudder novel.

EB   You've got a Scudder novel due out in the fall and a Bernie Rhoden-barr in the spring?

LB   Bernie probably in the spring. I don't even know who's publishing it at this moment. Next fall, assuming that I write a book this summer—and I intend to—will be the next Scudder book, as yet untitled. And the book after that will probably be the book about Keller, whenever that gets written—whenever it gets published. And after that, I have the luxury of not knowing.

EB   But you think you'll go on with Bernie?

LB At least for one more book; and I say that because I was asked. When we were offering the book to publishers, the question came up about how I felt about entering into a two-book contract, and I said I would be willing to commit to that.

EB Do you think that you would ever reach a point where you feel like you've said what you have to say and you're economically well off and you just don't want to write anymore?

LB I have probably long since said what I have to say. I don't know. Writers usually retire only when they write one or two more books than they should have and no one wants to publish them anymore or they just can't do it. I wouldn't have the problem so many people seem to have when they retire, of not knowing what to do with the days, because some of my days right now are not that different from a retiree's, and by writing, spending such a small portion of the year actually writing my work, that gives me a lot of practice in getting through the days the rest of the time.

If I retired, how would anyone know? It'd be hard to tell. I know I stopped writing certain series because it seemed to me that I'd done as much as I could with the idea. And someday that may be how I feel about fiction in general. I know it gets more and more difficult for me to read it. I just finish a small percentage of what I start, and that includes books I enjoy. Now, I don't know whether that will someday happen with the writing of it also, that entering into the world of the imagination that way will be just an auctorial pose.

It's impossible to say—to answer with assurance, one way or the other. I hope I can keep on doing this. I get enormous satisfaction out of it. I still get a kick out of seeing a new book. You'd think that pleasure would wear thin, but thus far it hasn't. I still get enormous satisfaction out of a growing body of work. I still believe, correctly or not, that my work is getting better. It's hard to know whether that's true or not, because I have a built-in bias to believe that. I always am fond of the book I just finished.

But I do think, from other people's reactions, that certainly in the Scudder series the books have gotten better in recent years. I would like for that to continue to happen. If it went the other direction, I don't know how much I'd want to go on writing, but I would probably be between the blinders of subjectivity and the great blessing of denial. I would probably be blissfully unaware of it.

The nightmare I have would be ending like Ross Macdonald, with Alzheimer's and the mind going. They say that for the person involved it's really only bad in the early portion of it, when you still realize what's happening, and then eventually you lose that, too. I would hate that. Ideally, I would like to live a very long time and be productive to the end. But we don't always get to choose what's next.

EB   Would it be a really big thing for you to make the best-seller list? Is that something that ever concerned you?

LB   Well, yes, actually I do want that. It's funny how nothing spurs ambition more than a little success. I find I'm rather more self-seeking in that regard after the success of the last couple of years than I was conscious of being before that. It's important to know that none of that matters, that it doesn't mean anything. It means something in money, which, in turn, doesn't really mean anything. But when I look at the best-seller list I'm not generally overcome with a desire to have written most of the books that are on it. There are always one or two books there that are pretty good stuff, but there's usually a dozen that are not. And certainly, they are not something I would have cared to have written.

I have had enough of a taste of that kind of popular success to have an appetite for more. However, if it never gets any better than it is now, I would not feel chagrined.

EB   You have won a number of awards, including several Edgars. I think it's a foregone conclusion that you will be an MWA [Mystery Writers of America] Grand Master before many more years.*

*Block did win the Grand Master in 1994.

LB I don't know about that. Awards are very gratifying to win, but they don't really mean a tremendous amount either. I guess nothing does but the work itself. I keep coming back to that.

Another thing that would certainly make retirement unpleasant is the extent to which doing the writing is just *necessary* for me, though it's obviously not something I have to do every day or every week or every month, but I have a feeling that it may be essential to my maintaining whatever equilibrium I have.

EB Most writers say they write because they feel like they have to. I mean, they're pushed to it; they're compelled to it. For many of the writers I know, that doesn't mean it's a pleasurable thing. They feel the isolation. They feel the struggle. It's painful. It's a constant giving birth. I get the sense from you that while it's hard work, generally speaking, you enjoy it.

LB I wouldn't take it quite that far. I enjoy having *done* it and I sometimes enjoy *doing* it. I've tried in recent years to enjoy the process more. I've always been very goal oriented, and when I'm writing a book, what I'm trying to do is complete it. It's important to have some motivation that way or you won't do it. At the same time, I can be so caught up in the desire to finish it that I don't enjoy the trip. I've tried to enjoy the process more, and I find I *am* enjoying the process more than I used to. One thing that amazes me—or used to amaze me—is that it never gets any easier. Now I think I've gotten used to the idea.

But it doesn't, and I suspect that if it does, then you're in big trouble, because that means you're not stretching enough. But to do my best work is as hard as it ever was, harder in some ways. I know that the first years that I wrote, I never threw anything away. I don't mean I kept it in a box in the closet. I mean, I finished and published—or finished and tried to publish—everything. Now when something's not going right I toss it, and I'm very glad of that. So standards do improve, but the writing itself is still difficult.

This last book I wrote while I was in San Francisco—it seems witless to insist that a book that was written in twenty-five days was that hard to write, but it was. And although I did work and get a sufficient amount done every day, it was a frightening experience for me. In fact, there were days I realized that I physically felt an almost paralyzing fear in my body because it was abundantly clear to me that the book couldn't possibly work out. That while there was a plot, I felt that I was throwing a lot of stuff out there—starting a lot of hares that were never going to get run down—that it just wouldn't make any sense at all.

It didn't make any sense to me. How was it possibly going to make any sense to anybody else? And when I'd reached the point where Bernie has them all in the room and says, "I suppose you're wondering why I summoned you all here," well, I don't know if they were wondering, but I was fucking well wondering, because I still didn't know how this was all going to work out.

Fortunately, fortunately, my character was smarter than I was, and he solved it. But I didn't know if he was going to, and that was scary. You know, for Christ's sake, I've been doing this for something like thirty-five years, and I've written God knows how many books. I've written a slew of mysteries. This is the sixth book about this character, and you would think I would know what I was doing. And you see, wannabes and lay people writing about the mystery genre talk about a formula as if there really is such a thing. As if there's something that makes it easy to do, and the truth is, there isn't anything that makes it easy to do. Writers don't have any formula. I don't, anyway. If I do, I'm unaware of it.

You have to invent the fucking wheel new each time, which is fine, I guess, if one wants a feeling of accomplishment in the end.

Sometimes the process itself is a delight. With that book I laughed aloud at the typewriter. I laughed aloud at it quite a few times. Whether anyone else will be similarly inclined, we don't know yet, but I had a great time.

When a scene comes to life—when it all gets down there almost as fast as your fingers can move—that's enormously satisfying. You know, I love it when it happens that way. Even when it's not that apparently effortless, it can still be very satisfying when you get it right. And I like the life very much.

EB On the down side, there are no guarantees, the writer has to expose himself to a great extent, there's the financial insecurity for an almost overwhelming majority of writers, there's the self-discipline that's involved, and there's the loneliness of writing being essentially a solitary occupation.

LB It's solitary—which is fine with me. I don't work or play well with others. There have been times when collaboration of one sort or another has been proposed; for example, screenwriting is ultimately a collaborative process, and it holds no attraction for me. I really don't want to work with others. I want to go into a room and come out and say, "Here it is," and for them to say, "This is perfect."

As far as financial security is concerned, I was fortunate to get into this when I was very young, when I couldn't have made any real money in anything else anyway, and I've learned to be comfortable in uncertain economic circumstances—or at least not as uncomfortable as one might be.

Self-discipline is another thing. People who aren't writers always tell writers how they really envy their self-discipline, and there's an implicit assumption there that if only they had it too, they could write best sellers. "I'd love to be a writer, you know. I wish I had your self-discipline, then I'd be one, you know." I don't know much about self-discipline. I can't make it come out if it's not there. I'm comfortable scheduling my time myself and not having someone else schedule it for me. I started doing all this so early that I didn't know better.

EB I have found over the years that a lot of talented people, not necessarily just writers, but actors, painters, and other creative folk, fail to make a career, or give it up, because they don't like that uncertainty and having to make all those decisions for themselves.

LB No question. No question. Anybody who's self-employed has the toughest boss in the world. There's no pleasing the son of a bitch. You don't get to leave it at the office, unless you learn how. I know of a man who could have been a free-lance writer and, in fact, he was for a little while. He stopped because he missed the social life at the office. Bored him to death, sitting in a room all day. He's bitched about his various jobs for the past thirty years and he's always said how he really wants to get back to free-lancing and he's always had a reason why he can't afford to. He's full of shit. He doesn't really want the life.

It's always priorities. The two things people say that always mean something else are: "I can't afford it" and "I don't have the time." They're just never true.

EB But it is scary in the sense that you're putting yourself on the line. You're baring your soul.

LB I'm not saying that they should do it. You learn how to deal with rejection. You just have to learn. People say, "I wish I had the time to write," and they say, "I wish I had your self-discipline." You never hear anybody say, "I would love to be a writer but I don't have the talent." Yet that's really what people don't have and what it's very difficult to do anything without. Now they don't have these illusions about being a major-league ballplayer. They don't say, "I would have been a major-league ballplayer but I didn't have the time." They know the reason was because they couldn't hit a curve ball.

EB In the introduction to one of your books about writing, you actually say something about that rather bluntly and honestly; that the people who subscribe to that magazine and others—the bulk of them—don't ever have a prayer. There's not a similar magazine for would-be ballplayers or would-be brain surgeons or, for that matter, even other people in the arts. I mean, I think that's kind of a unique thing. What is the appeal?

LB On the other hand, a lot of the people who are subscribing to *Writer's Digest* or any magazine like that *are* professionals or semiprofessionals.

They're not at the place they'd like to be with their writing. A lot of them are journalists or nonfiction writers who would like to be writing fiction—and some are. So, it's not entirely a "wanna-be" thing. Just as the people who come to Bouchercon are all fans but a great many of them have some professional or semiprofessional book interests—book selling or publishing or writing or journalism or whatever.

The thing is, with writing it's the fantasy, it's the dream life of a remarkable portion of the population. Heinlein once said that of every hundred readers, something like ninety-five are want-to-be writers. That's a little high—but it's not *that* high. An amazing proportion of people who come to signings manage, somewhere in the course of the little snippet of conversation, to volunteer that they've done some writing or they're trying to do some writing.

One thing I talk about in one of the columns is that writing ought to be an acceptable avocation. That there is a difference between the Sunday painter and the Sunday writer. Most people who paint don't have visions of gallery shows, but almost everybody who writes wants to be published.

EB So what compels writers, then?

LB Very simple. Writing isn't complete without publication. It doesn't seem like a complete act.

EB Without an audience?

LB That's really what it is, and it's not the same to give typewritten sheets to your friends. That's why we have the vanity presses. There's no equivalent in other areas.

You Can't Lose

ANYONE who starves in this country deserves it. Really. Almost anybody who is dumb enough to want to work can get a job without any back-breaking effort. Blindies and crips haul in twenty-five bucks an hour bumming the Times Square district. And if you're like me—able-bodied and all, but you just don't like to work, all you got to do is use your head a little. It's simple.

Of course, before you all throw up your jobs, let me explain that this routine has its limitations. I don't eat caviar, and East Third Street is a long way from Sutton Place. But I never cared much for caviar, and the pad I have is a comfortable one. It's a tiny room a couple blocks off the Bowery, furnished with a mattress, a refrigerator, a stove, a chair, and a table. The cockroaches get me out of bed, dress me, and walk me down to the bathroom down the hall. Maybe you couldn't live in a place like that, but I sort of like it. There's no problem keeping it up, 'cause it couldn't get any worse.

My meals, like I said, are not caviar. For instance, in the refrigerator right now I have a sack of coffee, a dozen eggs, and part of a fifth of bourbon. Every morning I have two fried eggs and a cup of coffee. Every evening I have three fried eggs and two cups of coffee. I figure, you find something you like, you should stick with it.

And the whole thing is cheap. I pay twenty a month for the room, which is cheap anywhere and amazing in New York. And in this neighborhood food prices are pretty low too.

All in all, I can live on ten bucks a week with no trouble. At the moment I have fifty bucks in my pocket, so I'm set for a month, maybe a little more. I haven't worked in four months, haven't had any income in three.

I live, more or less, by my wits. I hate to work. What the hell, what good are brains if you have to work for a living? A cat lives fifty, sixty, maybe seventy years, and that's not a long time. He might as well spend his time doing what he likes. Me, I like to walk around, see people, listen to music, read, drink, smoke, and get a dame. So that's what I do. Since nobody's paying people to walk around or read or anything, I pick up some gold when I can. There's always a way.

By this I don't mean that I'm a mugger or a burglar or anything like that. It might be tough for you to get what I'm saying, so let me explain.

I mentioned that I worked four months ago, but I didn't say that I only held the job for a day. It was at a drugstore on West Ninety-sixth Street. I got a job there as a stock and delivery boy on a Monday morning. It was easy enough getting the job. I reported for work with a couple of sandwiches in a beat-up gym bag. At four that afternoon I took out a delivery and forgot to come back. I had twenty shiny new Zippo lighters in the gym bag, and they brought anywhere from a buck to a buck-seventy-five at the Third Avenue hockshops. That was enough money for three weeks, and it took me all of one day to earn it. No chance of him catching me, either. He's got a fake name and a fake address, and he probably didn't notice the lighters were missing for a while.

Dishonest? Obviously, but so what? The guy deserved it. He told me straight off the Puerto Ricans in the neighborhood were not the cleverest mathematicians in the world, and when I made a sale I should shortchange them and we'd split fifty-fifty. Why should I play things straight with a bum like that? He can afford the loss. Besides, I worked one day free for him, didn't I?

It's all a question of using your head. If you think things out carefully, decide just what you want, and find a smart way to get it, you come out ahead, time after time. Like the way I got out of going into the army.

The army, as far as I'm concerned, is strictly for the sparrows. I couldn't see it a year ago, and I still can't. When I got my notice I had to think fast. I didn't want to try faking the eye chart or anything like that, and I didn't think I would get away with a conscientious objector pitch. Anyway, those guys usually wind up in stir or working twice as hard as everybody else. When the idea came to me it seemed far too simple, but it worked. I got myself deferred for homosexuality.

It was a panic. After the physical I went in for the psychiatric, and I played the beginning fairly straight, only I acted generally hesitant.

Then the Doc asks, "Do you like girls?"

"Well," I blurt out, "only as friends."

"Have you ever gone with girls?"

"Oh, no!" I managed to sound somewhat appalled at the idea.

I hesitated for a minute or two, then admitted that I was homosexual. I was deferred, of course.

You'd think that everybody who really wanted to avoid the army would try this, but they won't. It's psychological. Men are afraid of being homosexual, or of having people think they're homosexual. They're even afraid of some skull doctor who never saw them before and never will see them again. So many people are so stupid, if you just act a little smart you can't miss. After the examination was over I spent some time with the whore who lives across the hall from me. No sense talking myself into anything. A cat doesn't watch out, he can be too smart, you know.

To get back to my story—the money from the Zippos lasted two weeks, and I was practically broke again. This didn't bother me, though. I just sat around the pad for a while, reading and smoking, and sure enough, I got another idea that I figured would be worth a few bucks. I showered and shaved, and made a half-hearted attempt at shining my shoes. I had some shoe polish from the drugstore. I had some room in the gym bag after the Zippos, so I stocked up on toothpaste, shoe polish, aspirins, and that kind of junk. Then I put on the suit that I keep clean for emergencies. I usually wear dungarees, but once a month I need a suit for something, so I always have it clean and ready. Then, with a tie on and my hair combed for a change, I looked almost human. I left the room, splurged fifteen cents for a bus ride, and got off at Third Avenue and Sixtieth Street. At the corner of Third and Fifty-ninth is a small semi-hockshop that I cased a few days before. They do more buying and selling than actual pawning, and there aren't too many competitors right in the neighborhood. Their stock is average—the more common and lower-priced musical instruments, radios, cameras, record players, and the cheap stuff—clocks, lighters, rings, watches, and so on. I got myself looking as stupid as possible and walked in.

There must be thousands of hockshops in New York, but there are only two types of clerks. The first is usually short, bald, and over forty. He wears suspenders, talks straight to the lower-class customers and kowtows to the others. Most of the guys farther downtown fit into this category. The other type is like the guy I drew: tall, thick black hair, light-colored suit, and a wide smile. He talks gentleman-to-gentleman with his upper-class customers and patronizingly to the bums. Of the two, he's usually more dangerous.

My man came on with the Johnny-on-the-spot pitch, ready and willing to serve. I hated him immediately.

"I'm looking for a guitar," I said, "preferably a good one. Do you have anything in stock at the moment?" I saw six or seven on the wall, but when you play it dumb, you play it dumb.

"Yes," he said. "Do you play guitar?" I didn't, and told him so. No point in lying all the time. But, I added, I was going to learn.

He picked one off the wall and started plucking the strings. "This is an excellent one, and I can let you have it for only thirty-five dollars. Would you like to pay cash or take it on the installment plan?"

I must have been a good actor, because he was certainly playing me for a mark. The guitar was a Pelton, and it was in good shape, but it never cost more than forty bucks new, and he had a nerve asking more than twenty-five. Any minute now he might tell me that the last owner was an old lady who only played hymns on it. I held back the laugh and plunked the guitar like a nice little customer.

"I like the sound. And the price sounds about right to me."

"You'll never find a better bargain." Now this was laying it on with a trowel.

"Yes, I'll take it." He deserved it now. "I was just passing by, and I don't have much money with me. Could I make a down payment and pay the rest weekly?"

He probably would have skipped the down payment. "Surely," he said. For some reason I've always disliked guys who say "surely." No reason, really. "How much would you like to pay now?"

I told him I was really short at the moment, but could pay ten dollars a week. Could I just put a dollar down? He said I could, but in that case the price would have to be forty dollars, which is called putting the gouge on.

I hesitated a moment for luck, then agreed. When he asked for identification I pulled out my pride and joy.

In a wallet that I also copped from that drugstore I have the best identification in the world, all phony and all legal. Everything in it swears up and down that my name is Leonard Blake and I live on Riverside Drive. I have a baptismal certificate that I purchased from a sharp little entrepreneur at our high school back in the days when I needed proof of age to buy a drink. I have a Social Security card that can't be used for identification purposes but always is, and an unapproved application for a driver's license. To get one of these you just go to the Bureau of Motor Vehicles and fill it out. It isn't stamped, but no pawnbroker ever noticed that. Then there are membership cards in everything from the Captain Marvel Club to the NAACP. Of course he took my buck and I signed some papers.

I made it next to Louie's shop at Thirty-fifth and Third. Louie and I know each other, so there's no haggling. He gave me fifteen for the guitar, and I let him know it wouldn't be hot for at least ten days. That's the way I like to do business.

Fifteen bucks was a week and a half, and you see how easy it was. And it's fun to shaft a guy who deserves it, like that sharp clerk did. But when I got back to the pad and read some old magazines, I got another idea before I even had a chance to start spending the fifteen.

I was reading one of those magazines that are filled with really exciting information, like how to build a model of the Great Wall of China around your house, and I was wondering what kind of damn fool would want to build a wall around his house, much less a Great Wall of China type wall, when the idea hit me. Wouldn't a hell of a lot of the same type of people like a Sheffield steel dagger, twenty-five inches long, an authentic copy of a twelfth-century relic recently discovered in a Bergdorf castle? And all this for only two bucks postpaid, no CODs? I figured they might.

This was a big idea, and I had to plan it just right. A classified in that type of magazine cost two dollars, a post office box cost about five for three months. I was in a hurry, so I forgot about lunch, and rushed across town to the Chelsea Station on Christopher Street, and Lennie Blake got himself a post office box. Then I fixed up the ad a little, changing "twenty-five inches" to "over two feet." And customers would please allow three weeks for delivery. I sent ads and money to three magazines, and took a deep breath. I was now president of Comet Enterprises. Or Lennie Blake was. Who the hell cared?

For the next month and a half I stalled on the rent and ate as little as possible. The magazines hit the stands after two weeks, and I gave people time to send in. Then I went west again and picked up my mail.

A hell of a lot of people wanted swords. There were about two hundred envelopes, and after I finished throwing out the checks and requests for information, I wound up with $196 and sixty-seven 3¢ stamps. Anybody want to buy a stamp?

See what I mean? The whole bit couldn't have been simpler. There's no way in the world they can trace me, and nobody in the post office could possibly remember me. That's the beauty of New York—so many people. And how much time do you think the cops will waste looking for a two-bit swindler? I could even have made another pick-up at the post office, but greedy guys just don't last long in this game. And a federal rap I need like a broken ankle.

Right now I'm 100 percent in the clear. I haven't heard a rumble on the play yet, and already Lennie Blake is dead—burned to ashes and flushed down the toilet. Right now I'm busy establishing Warren Shaw. I sign the name, over and over, so that I'll never make a mistake and sign the wrong name sometime. One mistake is above par for the course.

Maybe you're like me. I don't mean with the same fingerprints and all, but the same general attitudes. Do you fit the following general description: smart, coldly logical, content with coffee and eggs in a cold-water walk-up, and ready to work like hell for an easy couple of bucks? If that's you, you're hired. Come right in and get to work. You can even have my room. I'm moving out tomorrow.

It's been kicks, but too much of the same general pattern and the law of averages gets you. I've been going a long time, and one pinch would end everything. Besides, I figure it's time I took a step or two up the social ladder.

I had a caller yesterday, a guy named Al. He's an older guy, and hangs with a mob uptown on the West Side. He always has a cigar jammed into the corner of his mouth and he looks like a holdover from the twenties, but Al is a very sharp guy. We gassed around for awhile, and then he looked me in the eyes and chewed on his cigar.

"You know," he said, "we might be able to use you."

"I always work alone, Al."

"You'd be working alone. Two hundred a night."

I whistled. This was sounding good. "What's the pitch?"

He gave me the look again and chewed his cigar some more. "Kid," he said, "did you ever kill a man?"

Two hundred bucks for one night's work! What a perfect racket! Wish me luck, will you? I start tonight.

Outliving a Father

THIS past June 24 I turned fifty-two.

This is not ordinarily considered the most noteworthy of birthdays. If I were more of a cardplayer, I might perhaps see it as significant to have lived a year for every card in the deck. Otherwise, though, the number is nothing special.

It was special for me, however, because on that day I became older by a day than my father ever got to be. He died on the morning of December 17, 1960, the day before his fifty-second birthday.

Not surprisingly, I remember it well. I was twenty-two. I had married in March of that year, and since then had been living with my wife in an apartment on West Sixty-ninth Street. My wife was pregnant, and we were expecting our first child in the spring.

My parents were in Buffalo, living with my sister in the house I grew up in. The three of them had visited us sometime during the fall, staying for several days at a small hotel a few blocks from us.

It must have been around four that morning when the phone rang. It was my mother. My father had been rushed to the hospital, he had had some sort of attack, and the situation was grave. I hung up the phone knowing that he was going to die, and realizing that I had somehow known for months that he was going to die.

An hour or so later there was another call. This time the caller was Moe Cheplove, our family physician and my parents' longtime friend. My father was dead.

I cashed a check at the stationer around the corner and we caught a train to Buffalo. There I learned that my father had died of an aortic aneurysm, a balloon in the wall of the aorta which had ruptured. En route to the hospital he said to my mother, "I hope you find a better guy next time." In the hospital he joked with the nurses. And then he died.

It is not unlikely that he experienced some symptoms a day or two before he was stricken, and that he overlooked them. In any event, he seems to have known what was coming. As we prepared for the funeral, my mother asked several friends of his to serve as honorary pallbearers. She had filled five of the six slots, when a man she had never met, a Mr. Lutwack, came to her and specifically asked to be a pallbearer. "I told him yes," she said, "because I didn't know how to tell him no."

Later, when we cleaned out my father's desk, we found a list he had recently made, six names with no heading or explanation. The five men she had chosen as pallbearers were on the list, along with Mr. Lutwack.

What was my father to Mr. Lutwack, or Mr. Lutwack to my father? It seems inescapable that, anticipating his own death, he had roughed out a list of pallbearers. He must have had some sort of conversation with Mr. Lutwack that prompted the man's request.

I could have asked Mr. Lutwack. I never did. I saw him only at the funeral and never managed a word with him. I had heard my father speak of him only in the last year or so of his life, and gather that they were business friends, but I never pursued the matter.

I wept for my father, and mourned him, and then I went back to New York to resume work on a novel and prepare for my daughter's birth. Within the first six months after my father's death I had a dream, all of it forgotten upon awakening. All, that is, but a date, and that date uncertain. It was either June 14, 1963, or June 13, 1964, and it was to be the date of my own death.

How seriously did I take the dream's warning? That's hard to say. I knew that dreams were often nonsense, that premonitions in real life (if not in fiction) usually came to nothing. Still, I knew that the ways of the world were mysterious, and that God gave every sign of having a sense of humor, and a mean streak. I don't think I did anything differently for having had the dream, but it was often on my mind.

And that's where it stayed. I never said anything to anyone. I had several close friends, but I never mentioned it to them, not even in the long whiskey-oiled conversations that characterized our evenings together. Nor did I ever say a word to my wife. I kept it all to myself, and waited.

The first date came and went. I was relieved, but it would be another year before I was out of the woods. And then, somewhere during that year, I forgot all about it. The whole thing left my consciousness, not to return until the fateful day had come and gone.

Almost twenty more years would pass before I mentioned the incident to anyone. (The man I told was astonished, swearing that the very same thing had happened to him, even to the two dates; he had never told anyone, either.) It was not until this year that I saw the link between my father's death and my dream. It seems obvious that it had sprung from a new awareness of mortality, but I never made the connection.

My sister died at thirty-five; two of my six first cousins, both younger than I, are gone. By the time I turned fifty I was a grandfather, and was suddenly seeing myself as part of an older generation. But it was the birthday two years later that brought the sound of Time's winged chariot hurrying near. My father, lighting the way for me, had lit it this far and no further. I did not need a dream to see my own death hovering in the shadows.

I forgave my father for dying, forgave him too for having left no last message, nothing but the cryptic list of six names. And I told myself I would show no lack of filial piety in outliving him.

The birthday came. I lived through it. Now I can even write about it.

Geographic Cures

IN the summer of 1975, shortly after my thirty-seventh birthday, I sold most of my possessions and gave up my Manhattan apartment. I piled my remaining goods into a rust-plagued Ford wagon and drove to Buffalo, where I moved in with a woman friend. I had everything just about unpacked when she came to me, looking troubled.

"I don't think this is working out," she said.

"Now you tell me," I said.

I repacked my things and stowed them in my mother's attic. Then I tried to figure out what to do next. I had reached the end of a couple of ropes, one personal and one professional. Two years ago I had had a wife and three daughters and a large farmhouse on twenty-two acres of rolling countryside, along with a shelf full of published books. Now I had a car and a typewriter and was unsure of my ability to point either of them in the right direction.

I didn't want to go back to New York. I didn't want to stay in Buffalo. A friend urged me to come to Los Angeles. "I guess I will," I said. "But it may take me a while to get there."

It took me nine months. If I didn't have any place to live, it struck me that the answer might lie in not living anywhere. A rolling stone gathered no moss, I told myself, and a moving target was harder to hit. I would head in the general direction of Los Angeles, and I would not stop anywhere en route for more than a month, and I would try to leave any stopping place before officially requested to do so.

I spent a month in Rodanthe, on North Carolina's Outer Banks. A fishing pier there stretched out into the Atlantic, and all day long people lined it, pulling in spot and croaker and flounder. Farm families flocked to the Banks in the fall; with the tobacco harvest in, they set about harvesting the sea, filling ice chests with fish that would carry them through the winter. I learned to fish that month, and I literally subsisted on what I pulled out of the ocean. I filleted my catch every night, rolled it in cornmeal and fried it in corn oil, dined well and had enough left over for breakfast the next morning.

For variety I sometimes crossed the island to the bay side and caught eels. The harbor there was full of commercial fishing boats, the fishermen a desperate-looking lot. We ignored each other, until one afternoon one of them hailed me. "I know ye're a Yankee," he said, "but do ye at least drink whiskey?"

"Only thing to do with it," I said.

We sat in his trailer and drank his whiskey and he asked me what on earth I did with eels. I fricasseed them, I said, as you might do with chicken. He shook his head at the thought of it.

From the Outer Banks I headed inland, to Greenville, South Carolina. Then I returned to the coast and spent several weeks in Charleston. There were no cheap hotels, but I found a rooming house downtown on Fulton Street. My room was twenty dollars a week, and a squalid little cell it was.

I went to Jekyll Island, Georgia, and St. Augustine and Naples, Florida. Mobile. Sardis, Mississippi. Looking for the bridge across the Mississippi, I misread a detour sign and wound up on a farm road that ran out in the middle of a plowed field, with the station wagon sunk up to its hubcaps in red clay. I got it out, and found the bridge, and crossed the river . . .

Wherever I went I was a tourist. I toured the battleship North Carolina in Wilmington harbor, the art museum in Greenville, and no end of historical sites in Charleston. Periodically I set up my typewriter on a motel desk and tried writing something. There is almost always a mirror hanging above the desk in a motel room, and the last thing one wants to look at, when stuck in pursuit of *le mot juste,* is one's own face.

Nor was my emotional state conducive to successful literary enterprise. I kept getting forty or fifty or sixty pages into a book and then having to abandon it because I couldn't see any reason for any of the characters involved to go on. I couldn't think of too many reasons to go on myself, for that matter, but something kept me moving. To Henrietta, Oklahoma. To Roswell, New Mexico. To Los Angeles.

There I lived for six months at the Magic Hotel, in Hollywood. My daughters flew out to spend the summer with me. They stayed at my hotel for a month, and then we took another month to drive east to New York. When we got there I found a place to park the car, took an apartment on Bleecker Street, and settled in.

I had had what I suppose you could call a midlife crisis, and by the time I was back in New York I seemed to have muddled through it. There was a point, during my sojourn at the Magic Hotel, when my circumstances had me seriously considering a life of crime. I determined that burglary best suited my solitary temperament, and I worked at opening the door to my hotel room without the key. I never got good enough at this to try turning the fantasy into reality, but before long I did something better with the fantasy; I started a book with a burglar as its hero. Back east I finished *Burglars Can't Be Choosers,* which turned out to be the first of five books about Bernie Rhodenbarr.

I was home again, and writing again, and once again selling what I wrote. I had successfully applied a geographic cure to a non-geographic problem.

It was not the last time I would do this.

In May of 1981 I got on a Greyhound bus late one night headed for Columbus, Ohio. I had a knapsack and a copy of *Running Times* magazine, and I didn't know when I'd be back.

Another relationship had gone to hell. I had been living with a woman for three and a half years and we had agreed to split up, and that she would retain the apartment. I had no place to live, and no compelling reason to rush to find new quarters, or to spend the summer in the city.

And I had what Joni Mitchell has called the urge for going. In recent years I had taken up running, and indeed had just returned from a marathon in Madrid. There were races to be run every weekend, closer than Madrid but further than Central Park. Of the contiguous forty-eight states, I had been to all but four. I could route myself through the ones I'd missed, and could contrive to be in the right place for a race on the weekend. I no longer owned a car, but Greyhound would take me wherever I wanted to go, and I could dope out my route as I went along.

In Chicago I stayed at the Y and ran in the Zoo Run in Lincoln Park. In Iowa City I stayed at a youth hostel, where a fellow visitor understood the uses of travel as a means of recovery from a punctured romance. It took time to get over these things, he said. His own marriage had broken up a while ago, and he still wasn't ready to resume his life.

I asked how long it had been. "Almost six years," he said, "and I'm starting to make real progress, but you can't rush these things."

I ran in a five-miler in Ft. Dodge, Iowa, and caught a ride to Sioux Falls, where I stayed at the Bus Hotel. I spent a week at the Malinda Motel, in Brookings, South Dakota, then hitchhiked to Clark, where they were celebrating their centennial. There were no rooms to be had so I slept in the park and ran in a 10-K race the next morning. A week later I was in Grand Forks, running in the North Dakota marathon, thirteen miles out and thirteen miles back, straight as a die and flat as a fritter.

I had never been in Iowa before, or North Dakota. Or Montana, where I went next, staying in Billings and Great Falls and Missoula. Or Idaho, which I crossed on a night bus to Portland via Spokane. I ran in a half-marathon in Cottago Grove, Oregon, then stayed at a Presbyterian hostel in Coos Bay. I ran in the Gay Run in San Francisco and a hospital benefit run in L.A., where I picked up a quickie screenwriting assignment and made enough money to fly home. A good thing, too, as I had just about had it with buses.

And, back in the city, I was ready to take up my life again. I had been to interesting places and met interesting people, and I had the T-shirts to prove it, souvenirs of the races I'd run. I hadn't solved any of the problems I'd spent the summer running away from, but I had successfully postponed dealing with them, and now I seemed able to do so.

Shortly after my return, in September of '81, I met a woman named Lynne Wood. The following July we began keeping company, and in October of '83 we were married. A native of New Orleans, Lynne, like me, had spent all her adult life in New York. After two idyllic years of married life in Greenwich Village, we gave up our apartment and moved to Ft. Myers Beach, Florida.

After two years it was clear that we had made a mistake. All its charms notwithstanding, the Gulf Coast was emphatically Nor For Us. But we were by no means certain that we wanted to return to New York, nor did we feel sanguine about pulling up stakes only to set them down in some other unknown spot.

For years we had entertained the fantasy of traveling without a destination, of living on the road. It struck us that we would never have a better opportunity to live out that fantasy. We would close the house and commit ourselves to two years as nomads, after which time we would know what we wanted to do next.

Lynne found a focus for the trip. Earlier I had been researching a novel called *Random Walk* (itself concerned with people ambling aimlessly across America) and had discovered that there were far more towns and hamlets named Buffalo than I had ever realized, something like twenty of them at rough count. "On our travels," I suggested, "we might go to some of them."

Lynne said, "I think we should go to *all* of them."

There were, as it turned out, rather more than twenty Buffalos. We have thus far been to fifty-eight, and know of twenty-three others. The Buffalo hunt gave the illusion of purpose to our two years on the road, but even without that direction I can't imagine a better way we could have spent those years. We rode horses in West Texas and rafted a river in Colorado. We stayed for a month in Sedona, Arizona, in a rented condo, and for six weeks in a cottage outside of Santa Fe, and we occasionally relied for shelter upon the kindness of acquaintances, but mostly we stayed in motels. We explored national parks—Grand Canyon, Big Bend, Guadalupe, Zion, Glacier. Lynne spent one September in New York while I holed up in a writers' colony in Virginia to write a book. We headed west, and were traipsing through Arches National Park while my agent conducted a spirited auction with the manuscript.

"From now on," Lynne said, "whenever you have a book to auction, we're coming to Moab, Utah. This place is lucky for us."

We are back in New York now, but it doesn't feel as though our travels have ended. On the contrary, it seems likely that we have learned the knack of traveling without a destination, of seeking geographic cures even in the absence of a problem, geographic or otherwise. Next summer we plan to walk across Spain, following the old pilgrims' route over the Pyrenees to Santiago de Compostela. And when we return, well, there will always be another Buffalo to track down. *So many Buffalos,* Lynne's sweatshirt says. *So many Buffalos, so little time. . . .*

The Lure of New Places

IN our prenuptial days, at a time when a more firmly grounded couple might have been picking a china pattern or names for the baby, Lynne and I decided to make a list of places we'd like to visit. After an exhilarating couple of minutes it became clear that we were on a fool's errand. All we were doing was writing down the name of every country we could think of. San Marino? Senegal? Sri Lanka? Sure, why not? If we hadn't been there, we wanted to go.

Now nine years have passed, albeit in the wink of an eye. My life list, as an ornithologist might call it, stands at thirty-one countries and forty-eight states, and my eagerness to extend it shows no sign of abating. Each new trip only fuels the fire.

Here's an example. We spent this past August on the southern Silk Road, in the remote reaches of western China. Our group went where no Americans had ever gone before, and visited towns and villages where no one had ever seen a Westerner, or a fork, or a toilet. The trip was quite wonderful, but that's not all it was, and, as Dr. Johnson said of *Paradise Lost*, no one would have wished it longer.

Afterward, jet lag hung on like grim death. I knew it was over when two things happened one right after the other. I got the first full night's sleep in three weeks, and I reached for an adventure travel catalogue and read it with a quickening pulse.

Why, I wonder, do I feel this urgent need to go everywhere? Given my

149

intense and perhaps unwarranted love for the city I live in, why am I so eager to leave it to go anywhere at all? What do I get out of it?

Several answers occur to me:

1. *Every new place gives me more of a handle on the world.* Five years ago Lynne and I spent three weeks in West Africa, visiting Senegal, Togo, Ivory Coast and Mali. By the time we returned, our sense of the planet was vastly changed. On our own internal globes, those four countries were now illuminated, and they cast a pale glow as well over the rest of the Dark Continent. Africa had become a part of our world in a way it had not previously been.

A destination does not have to be exotic in order to enlarge the world for me. When a business trip took us to Omaha in May, Lynne and I took an extra week to drive all around the state of Nebraska. We had logged the state some years back, but had never had a chance to explore it. We drove through the sandhill country, climbed Scott's Bluff, and gazed in wild surmise at Carhenge, a precise recreation of Stonehenge constructed of ruined and spray-painted old automobiles. (Lynne says the natives use it to predict the Mitsubishi Eclipse.)

Now we own Nebraska. It's part of our world, and our world is larger for it.

2. *I'm a writer and I need material.* Nice try, huh? It's undeniably true that writers from Somerset Maugham to Paul Theroux have roamed the world and come back with stories. It's also true that every few years I actually write a short story with a foreign setting. But what I mostly do, after ranging compulsively all over the globe, is come home and hole up and write yet another crime novel set in the gritty streets of New York.

That said, I would still contend that the travel plays a role in the creative process. Perhaps it lets me see my home turf more vividly. Or maybe it just shakes things up a little.

Once, during a sleepless night on a ghastly train ride from Luxor to Cairo, I figured out exactly how to write a novel that had stumped me for a couple of years. And in August, bouncing around on a Bactrian camel in China's Taklamakan desert, scanning the horizon for signs of the Lost City of Karadung, I came up with an idea for the book I'll write next.

Would either of these ideas have come to me in an easy chair in, say, Saugerties? Somehow I doubt it. On the other hand, I've never been to Saugerties . . .

3. *Destinations make the ideal collection.* For years I collected things. Stamps. Coins. Rocks. Books. Empty liquor bottles. (Don't ask.)

Collections are a burden. They take up space. They have to be displayed and dusted and fussed over. Either they're valueless, in which case you feel like an idiot for treasuring them, or they're valuable and they'll get stolen. Either way they own you more than you own them, and when you finally die they're one more thing for your kids to throw out.

I'd rather collect experiences. Blissfully maintenance-free, they can only go up in value. They don't take up any space, and when I'm gone they'll go with me.

I've been to thirty-one countries. I've been to forty-eight states. I've been to sixty-five towns named Buffalo. That's my collection, and every item in it is a favorite.

4. *Why ask why?* The nice thing about compulsive behavior is that you don't have to explain it. Which is just as well, because you can't.

There is, I am told, a fraternal organization for compulsive globetrotters, its members united by the obsessive desire to visit every last one of the 300-plus countries and territories in the world. Just thinking of the task, I know how the young Thomas Wolfe felt when it dawned on him that he could never hope to read all the books in the library, or sleep with all the beautiful women in New York, or even know Brooklyn, not really, not through and through. I might someday amass the 100 countries required for membership, but a complete collection would appear to be beyond anybody's reach.

Nor would it truly scratch the itch. Mali's on my life list, but I'll have to go back; I didn't get to Timbuctoo, and I want to. A trip to Rajasthan last year put India on my list and left me knowing I'll have to make six or eight more trips to the subcontinent in order to feel I own it. An overnight stay at Narita on the way home from China let me put a check mark next to Japan, but it also left me resolved to spend at least a month in the country. I haven't been anywhere in Eastern Europe yet, and every time I look at the map there are more countries there, singing their siren song.

Not long ago I read a newspaper article about a chap no madder than I who had just completed the work of a lifetime. He had set foot in every county in all fifty states.

"What a crazy thing to do," I said to Lynne.

"Completely nuts," she agreed. "How many counties are there, anyway?"

"In round numbers," I said, "3102."

"No kidding."

"Delaware has only three."

"That's not many."

"Texas," I added, "is blessed with 254."

"It would be easy to knock off Delaware," she mused, "but Texas would be murder."

"We probably already have a good chunk of Texas," I said. "We've driven across it, what, half a dozen times? And we've taken a different route every time. I wonder."

"You wonder what?"

"Oh," I said, "I was just wondering how many counties we've been to. That's all."

"Oh, no," she said. "Here we go again."

A Modest Proposal for the Categorization of Mysteries

SEVERAL times in recent years there has been agitation for the establishment of official categories within the overall field of mystery fiction, especially in respect to awards. The argument has been advanced that a system which simply recognizes a "best" annual novel for the entire field is apt to lean toward books of a certain stripe and slight others which, while every bit as worthy, are horses of another color. Judges, one is given to understand, consistently favor the realistic over the romantic, the dark over the light, the serious over the frivolous, the hardboiled over the cozy, the yang over the yin.

There have been various attempts to rectify this situation. New organizations have sprung into being, each handing out an annual award for the best book in a particular category. *Mystery Scene* has established a whole slate of awards which divide the field into a host of subgenres. (I myself was greatly honored this past year when my book *Out on the Cutting Edge* was nominated for an award in the category of *Best Private Eye Novel with a New York Setting by a Male Writer Over 40;* I only wish I'd walked off with the prize, but, with so much great work being done in that subgenre, the nomination was honor enough.)

Mystery Writers of America has steadfastly resisted the pressure to establish categories of mystery fiction. The prevailing sentiment has always been that to do so would be to dilute the considerable prestige of the Edgar Allan Poe awards, which were established to honor the best work in the field without qualification. To establish a special award, say, for the year's best work of romantic suspense, would be to say in effect that the book in question would not merit recognition save in its particular category. To give such awards for the best juvenile mystery, the best paperback original, the best first novel, would not so demean the recipients, but to do so with subgenres would.

More recently, there has been increasing opinion favoring two categories—and a great deal of difficulty in determining just how those categories are to be defined. The best classic puzzle and the best realistic novel, the best hardboiled book and the best cozy, the best dark book and the best light book, the best serious book and the best comic novel. The best yin, that is to say, and the best yang.

The problem here, it seems to me, is how to decide what book belongs in what category. Hardly a month goes by that I don't read a classic puzzle which is also a hard-edged look at crime in modern times, or a tough book which is also humorous, or a fine piece of crime fiction which is at once dark and light, and all shades of gray in between. To require of an Edgar Awards committee or chairperson that he or she or they decide which nominated book is eligible for which award would place an impossible burden on a person or persons already overtaxed. To assign this chore to the various publishers who nominate the books would require such persons to be more familiar with the works they've published than they very often are. Even assuming the publishers have read the books, how good are they going to be in determining their place in categories we ourselves are hard-put to define?

Yet another suggestion, that an Edgar be given annually for Best Book by a Male Author and Best Book by a Female Author, hardly deserves comment.

It occurs to me that there may be an easy way to manage a fair solution. I would propose two categories, so composed that one may determine instantly and without argument into which category any given book ought to be consigned.

To wit: Books With Cats and Books Without Cats.

The boundaries of these two subgenres are, it seems to me, quite perfectly defined. A book either has a cat in it or it does not. The role the cat plays—i.e., whether it solves the crime or merely crosses the hero's path—is immaterial. If there's a cat in the book, in any capacity whatsoever, the book is eligible for the Best Mystery With Cats award. If there's not, it's not.

At the same time, the distinction is not purely arbitrary. Books With Persian Rugs and Books Without Persian Rugs is every bit as clearcut, but serves no purpose. The cat, though, is a good litmus test for the mystery. It is true, to be sure, that there are cozies without cats, even as there are hardboiled books with them, but that's no problem. Imagine the fun when a novel by James Ellroy, say, wins Best Mystery With Cats.

I won't pursue this any further. It is, to be sure, very much a modest proposal, with a great deal to be modest about. My intent is merely to launch it among you and let it go where it will—to run it up a tree, as it were, and see if it can get down by itself. Meanwhile, I've got a book of my own to write.

Don't ask.

A Lawrence Block Bibliography

BOOKS

Lawrence Block

1961

Mona [novel]. Gold Medal Books [paperback]. Retitled and reissued as *Sweet Slow Death* (A Jove Book [paperback], 1986).

Death Pulls a Doublecross [novel]. Gold Medal Books [paperback]. Retitled and reissued as *Coward's Kiss* (Foul Play Press [paperback], 1987).

Markham "The Case of the Pornographic Photos" [novel]. Belmont Books [paperback]. Retitled and reissued as *You Could Call It Murder* (Foul Play Press [paperback], 1987).

1965

The Girl with the Long Green Heart [novel]. A Fawcett Gold Medal Book [paperback]. English edition: Hale [first hardcover edition], 1980.

1966

The Thief Who Couldn't Sleep [novel; first book in Evan Tanner series]. A Fawcett Gold Medal Book [paperback].

The Canceled Czech [novel; Tanner]. A Fawcett Gold Medal Book [paperback].

1967

Tanner's Twelve Swingers [novel]. A Fawcett Gold Medal Book[paperback].

Deadly Honeymoon [novel]. Macmillan Co. [first hardback book].

1968

Two for Tanner [novel]. A Fawcett Gold Medal Book [paperback].

Tanner's Tiger [novel]. A Fawcett Gold Medal Book [paperback].

Here Comes A Hero [novel; Tanner]. A Fawcett Gold Medal Book [paperback].

1969

> *The Specialists* [novel]. A Fawcett Gold Medal Book [paperback].
>
> *After the First Death* [novel]. Macmillan Co.

1970

> *Me Tanner, You Jane* [novel]. Macmillan Co.

1971

> *Ronald Rabbit Is a Dirty Old Man* [novel]. Bernard Geis Associates.

1976

> *The Sins of the Fathers* [novel; first book in Matthew Scudder series]. A Dell Book [paperback]. English edition: Hale [first hardcover edition], 1979. 1992 reissue: Dark Harvest, with introduction by Stephen King [in addition to the trade edition, a limited edition of 400 copies numbered and signed by the author and Stephen King was issued].
>
> *In the Midst of Death* [novel; Scudder]. A Dell Book [paperback]. English edition:
> Hale [first hardcover edition], 1979. 1994 reissue: Dark Harvest, with introduction by Martin Cruz Smith [in addition to the trade edition, a limited edition numbered and signed by the author and Martin Cruz Smith was issued].

1977

> *Time to Murder and Create* [novel; Scudder]. A Dell Book [paperback]. English edition: Hale [first hardcover edition], 1979. 1993 reissue: Dark Harvest, with introduction by Jonathan Kellerman [in addition to the trade edition, a limited edition of 300 copies numbered and signed by the author and Jonathan Kellerman was issued].
>
> *Burglars Can't Be Choosers* [novel; first book in Bernie Rhodenbarr series]. Random House [also sold with a special bookplate edition, limited to 1,000 copies, numbered and signed by the author].

1978

> *The Burglar in the Closet* [novel; Rhodenbarr]. Random House.

1979

> *The Burglar Who Liked to Quote Kipling* [novel; Rhodenbarr]. Random House.
>
> *Writing the Novel from Plot to Print* [nonfiction]. Writer's Digest Books.

1980

> *Mr. Rhodenbarr, Bookseller, Advises a Young Customer on Seeking a Vocation* [excerpt]. Oak Knoll Books [paperback; limited to 250 numbered copies]. Reprint of the first chapter of *The Burglar Who Liked to Quote Kipling*.

Ariel [novel]. Arbor House [also sold with a special bookplate edition, limited to 500 copies, numbered and signed by the author].

The Burglar Who Studied Spinoza [novel; Rhodenbarr]. Random House.

1981

A Stab in the Dark [novel; Scudder]. Arbor House.

Telling Lies for Fun & Profit: A Manual for Fiction Writers [nonfiction]. Arbor House, with introduction by Brian Garfield.

Real Food Places [nonfiction]. Rodale Press, written with Cheryl Morrison.

Code of Arms [novel]. Richard Marek Publishers, written with Harold King.

1982

Eight Million Ways to Die [novel; Scudder]. Arbor House.

1983

Sometimes They Bite [short stories]. Arbor House.

The Burglar Who Painted Like Mondrian [novel]. Arbor House.

1984

Like a Lamb to Slaughter [short stories]. Arbor House, with introduction by Joe Gores.

1985

Write for Your Life [nonfiction]. Published by Lawrence Block [5,000 copies].

1986

When the Sacred Ginmill Closes [novel; Scudder]. Arbor House.

1987

Into the Night [novel]. Mysterious Press, started by Cornell Woolrich and completed by Lawrence Block, with afterword by Francis M. Nevins, Jr.

Spider Spin Me a Web [nonfiction]. Writer's Digest Books.

1988

Random Walk [novel]. A Tor Book.

1989

Out on the Cutting Edge [novel; Scudder]. William Morrow and Co.

1990

A Ticket to the Boneyard [novel; Scudder]. William Morrow and Co.

1991

A Dance at the Slaughterhouse [novel; Scudder]. William Morrow and Co.

1992

A Walk Among the Tombstones [novel; Scudder]. William Morrow and Co.

1993

Some Days You Get the Bear [short stories]. William Morrow and Co.

The Devil Knows You're Dead [novel; Scudder]. William Morrow and Co.

1994.

The Burglar Who Traded Ted Williams [novel; Rhodenbarr]. Dutton.

Chip Harrison

1970

No Score [novel]. A Fawcett Gold Medal Book [paperback]. Reissued within *Introducing Chip Harrison* (Foul Play Press, 1984 [trade paperback]).

1971

Chip Harrison Scores Again [novel]. A Fawcett Gold Medal Book [paperback]. Reissued within *Introducing Chip Harrison* (Foul Play Press, 1984 [trade paperback]).

1974

Make Out with Murder [novel]. A Fawcett Gold Medal Book [paperback]. Reissued within *A/K/A Chip Harrison* (Foul Play Press, 1983 [trade paperback]). Retitled and reissued in England as *Five Little Rich Girls* (Allison & Busby, 1984 [first hardcover edition]).

1975

The Topless Tulip Caper [novel]. A Fawcett Gold Medal Book [paperback]. English edition: Allison & Busby [first hardcover edition], 1984. Reissued within *A/K/A Chip Harrison* (Foul Play Press, 1983 [trade paperback]).

1983

A/K/A Chip Harrison [novels]. Foul Play Press [trade paperback]. Reprint of *Make Out with Murder* and *The Topless Tulip Caper.*

1984

Introducing Chip Harrison [novels]. Foul Play Press [trade paperback]. Reprint of *No Score* and *Chip Harrison Scores Again.*

Paul Kavanagh

1969

Such Men Are Dangerous [novel]. Macmillan Co.

1971

The Triumph of Evil [novel]. World Publishing Co.

1974

Not Comin' Home to You [novel]. G. P. Putnam's Sons.

SHORT STORIES

1958

"You Can't Lose." *Manhunt.* February 1958.

"A Fire in the Night." *Manhunt.* June 1958.

"The Way to Power." *Trapped Detective Stories.* June 1958.

"The Dope." *Guilty Detective Story Magazine.* July 1958.

"Murder Is My Business." *Off Beat Detective Story Magazine.* September 1958.

"Lie Back and Enjoy It." *Trapped Detective Stories.* October 1958.

"The Bad Night." *Guilty Detective Story Magazine.* November 1958.

[as B. L. Lawrence] "One Night of Death." *Guilty Detective Story Magazine.* November 1958.

"Ride a White Horse." *Manhunt.* December 1958.

1959

"The Burning Fury." *Off Beat Detective Stories.* April 1959.

"Look Death in the Eye." *Saturn Web Detective Stories.* April 1959.

"Bride of Violence." *Two Fisted Detective Stories.* December 1959.

1961

"I Don't Fool Around." *Trapped Detective Stories.* February 1961.

"Package Deal." *Ed McBain's Mystery Magazine.* Issue no. 3 [publication's last issue].

1962

"A Shroud for the Damned." *Keyhole Mystery Magazine.* April 1962.

"Frozen Stiff." *Manhunt.* June 1962.

1963

"If This Be Madness." *Alfred Hitchcock's Mystery Magazine.* January 1963. In *Like a Lamb to Slaughter* (1984).

"The Books Always Balance." *Alfred Hitchcock's Mystery Magazine.* July 1963. In *Alfred Hitchcock's Tales to Scare You Stiff* (1979).

"Good for the Soul." *Alfred Hitchcock's Mystery Magazine.* August 1963. In *The Second Black Lizard Anthology of Crime Fiction* (1988).

1964

"When This Man Dies." *Alfred Hitchcock's Mystery Magazine.* April 1964. In *Alfred*

Hitchcock's Borrowers of the Night (1983). Adapted for the television program "Alfred Hitchcock Presents."

1966

"With a Smile for the Ending." *Alfred Hitchcock's Mystery Magazine.* January 1966. In *Alfred Hitchcock's Tales to Send Chills Down Your Back* (1979). Magazine changed title to "Bits and Pieces."

"Passport in Order." *Alfred Hitchcock's Mystery Magazine.* February 1966. In *Alfred Hitchcock's A Choice of Evils* (1983).

"Pseudo Identity." *Alfred Hitchcock's Mystery Magazine.* November 1966. In *Alfred Hitchcock's Tales to Be Read with Caution* (1980).

"Some Things a Man Must Do." *Alfred Hitchcock's Mystery Magazine.* December 1966. In *Some Days You Get the Bear* (1993).

1967

"Death Wish." *Alfred Hitchcock's Mystery Magazine.* March 1967. In *Alfred Hitchcock Presents: A Month of Mystery* (1969).

"The Most Unusual Snatch." *Alfred Hitchcock's Mystery Magazine.* April 1967. In *Alfred Hitchcock's Tales to Make You Weak in the Knees* (1982).

1974

"That Kind of Day." *Alfred Hitchcock's Mystery Magazine.* June 1974. In *Alfred Hitchcock's Tales to Make Your Teeth Chatter* (1981).

"The Gentle Way." *Alfred Hitchcock's Mystery Magazine.* July 1974. In *Sometimes They Bite* (1983).

1976

"Sometimes They Bite." *Alfred Hitchcock's Mystery Magazine.* June 1976. In *Sometimes They Bite* (1983).

"Funny You Should Ask." *Alfred Hitchcock's Mystery Magazine.* August 1976. In *Sometimes They Bite* (1983). Magazine changed title to "A Pair of Recycled Jeans."

"The Dettweiler Solution." *Alfred Hitchcock's Mystery Magazine.* September 1976. In *Alfred Hitchcock's Tales to Take Your Breath Away* (1978).

1977

"Strangers on a Handball Court." *Alfred Hitchcock's Mystery Magazine.* January 1977. In *Sometimes They Bite* (1983).

"Nothing Short of Highway Robbery." *Alfred Hitchcock's Mystery Magazine.* March 1977. In *Sometimes They Bite* (1983).

"A Bad Night for Burglars." *Ellery Queen's Mystery Magazine.* April 1977. In

Ellery Queen's Maze of Mysteries (1982). Magazine changed title to "Gentleman's Agreement."

"Like a Dog in the Street." *Alfred Hitchcock's Mystery Magazine.* April 1977. In *Sometimes They Bite* (1983).

"This Crazy Business of Ours." *Alfred Hitchcock's Mystery Magazine.* May 1977. In *Sometimes They Bite* (1983). Magazine changed title to "This Crazy Business."

"The Dangerous Business." *Ellery Queen's Mystery Magazine.* June 1977. In *Like a Lamb to Slaughter* (1984). Original title was "The Dangerous Game."

"Collecting Ackermans." *Alfred Hitchcock's Mystery Magazine.* July 1977. In *Sometimes They Bite* (1983).

"Out the Window." *Alfred Hitchcock's Mystery Magazine.* September 1977. In *Sometimes They Bite* (1983). Features Matthew Scudder.

"Like a Lamb to Slaughter." *Alfred Hitchcock's Mystery Magazine.* November 1977. In *Like a Lamb to Slaughter* (1984). Author changed the title from "A Candle for the Bag Lady" to make it the title story for the collection.

"Click!" *Alfred Hitchcock's Mystery Magazine.* December 1977. In *Like a Lamb to Slaughter* (1984).

1978

"Change of Life." *Alfred Hitchcock's Mystery Magazine.* January 1978. In *Like a Lamb to Slaughter* (1984).

"The Ehrengraf Defense." *Ellery Queen's Mystery Magazine.* February 1978. In *Sometimes They Bite* (1983). Original title was "The Ehrengraf Method."

"One Thousand Dollars a Word." *Alfred Hitchcock's Mystery Magazine.* March 1978. In *Sometimes They Bite* (1983).

"The Ehrengraf Presumption." *Ellery Queen's Mystery Magazine.* May 1978.

"The Ehrengraf Experience." *Ellery Queen's Mystery Magazine.* August 1978. In *Like a Lamb to Slaughter* (1984).

"Weekend Guests." *Alfred Hitchcock's Mystery Magazine.* August 1978. In *Like a Lamb to Slaughter* (1984).

"And Miles to Go Before I Sleep." *Alfred Hitchcock's Mystery Magazine.* October 1978. In *Sometimes They Bite* (1983). Original title was "Life after Life."

"The Ehrengraf Appointment." *Mike Shane's Mystery Magazine.* December 1978. In *Like a Lamb to Slaughter* (1984).

"The Ehrengraf Riposte." *Ellery Queen's Mystery Magazine.* December 1978. In *Ellery Queen's 11 Deadly Sins* (1989).

1979

"The Ehrengraf Obligation." *Ellery Queen's Mystery Magazine*. March 1979. In
Sometimes They Bite (1983).

"You Could Call It Blackmail." *For Women Only*. In *Like a Lamb to Slaughter*
(1984).

1981

"A Little Off the Top." *Gallery*. May 1981. In *Like a Lamb to Slaughter* (1984).

"Going through the Motions." *Ellery Queen's Mystery Magazine*. August 1981. In
Sometimes They Bite (1983).

1982

"Hot Eyes, Cold Eyes." *Gallery*. February 1982. In *Like a Lamb to Slaughter*
(1984).

"The Ehrengraf Alternative." *Ellery Queen's Mystery Magazine*. September 1982.
In *Some Days You Get the Bear* (1993).

1983

"Like a Thief in the Night." *Cosmopolitan*. May 1983. In *Like a Lamb to Slaughter*
(1984). Features Bernie Rhodenbarr.

1984

"The Ehrengraf Nostrum." *Ellery Queen's Mystery Magazine*. May 1984. In *Some
Days You Get the Bear* (1993).

"By the Dawn's Early Light." *Playboy*. August 1984. In *Some Days You Get the
Bear* (1993). Winner of the Shamus and Edgar Allan Poe Awards. Features
Matthew Scudder.

"The Boy Who Disappeared Clouds." *Magazine of Fantasy and Science Fiction*.
December 1984. In *Like a Lamb to Slaughter* (1984).

"Death of the Mallory Queen." In *Like a Lamb to Slaughter* (1984). Features Chip
Harrison.

"Leo Youngdahl, R.I.P." In *Like a Lamb to Slaughter* (1984).

1985

"Like a Bug on a Windshield." *Ellery Queen's Mystery Magazine*. October 1985. In
Some Days You Get the Bear (1993).

1986

"As Good as a Rest." *Ellery Queen's Mystery Magazine*. August 1986. In *Scarlet
Letters* (1991).

1989

"Cleveland in My Dreams." *Ellery Queen's Mystery Magazine*. February 1989. In
Some Days You Get the Bear (1993).

"The Burglar Who Dropped in on Elvis." *Playboy.* April 1990. In *Some Days You Get the Bear* (1993). Features Bernie Rhodenbarr.

"Answers to Soldier." *Playboy.* June 1990. In *Some Days You Get the Bear* (1993). Nominated for the Edgar Allan Poe Award. Features Keller.

1991

"Something to Remember You By." *New Mystery.* July/August 1991. In *Some Days You Get the Bear* (1993).

"A Blow for Freedom." *Playboy.* October 1991. In *The Year's Best Mystery and Suspense Stories 1992* (1992), edited by Edward D. Hoch. Nominated for the Edgar Allan Poe Award.

1992

"Hilliard's Ceremony." *Armchair Detective.* Summer 1992. In *Some Days You Get the Bear* (1993).

"Batman's Helpers." In *Justice for Hire: Private Eye Writers of America* (1992). Features Matthew Scudder.

1993

"How Would You Like It?" In *Psycho-Paths II* (1993), edited by Robert Bloch and Martin H. Greenberg.

"The Merciful Angel of Death." In *The New Mystery, Original Anthology of the International Association of Crime Writers* (1993). Features Matthew Scudder.

"Keller's Therapy." *Playboy.* May 1993.

"Someday I'll Plant More Walnut Trees." In *Some Days You Get the Bear* (1993).

"Some Days You Get the Bear." In *Some Days You Get the Bear* (1993).

"The Tulsa Experience." In *Some Days You Get the Bear* (1993).

In press

"Dogs Walked, Plants Watered." *Playboy.*

"Keller on Horseback." In *Mickey Spillane's Murder Is My Business.*